Praise for *Give Me a Break*

"Discover the negative beliefs that stop you from enjoying your life and managing your time. A great read and very practical."

—Shelle Rose Charvet, author, *The Customer is Bothering Me*

"A fantastic resource aimed at people who are losing the battle with the clock."

—Tod Maffin, Digital Marketing Strategist

"If this book doesn't help you manage your time better . . . NOTHING WILL!"

—Jason Parker, Olympic Medalist, International Speaker & Entrepreneur

"*Give Me a Break* is about more than just time management: Culver will help you with life management."

—Laura Stack, author, *SuperCompetent*

GIVE ME A
BREAK

The art of making *time* work for *you*

Hugh D. Culver

Kaire Publishing
Canada

Library and Archives Canada Cataloguing in Publication

Culver, Hugh D., 1958–

Give me a break : the art of making time work for you / written by Hugh D. Culver ; illustrations by Sandy Magee ; cartoons by Randy Glasbergen.

ISBN 978-0-9867656-1-2 (bound).—ISBN 978-0-9867656-0-5 (pbk).

1. Time management. 2. Work-life balance. I. Title.

HD69.T54C84 2011   650.1'1   C2010-907608-7

Proofreading by Diana Alfred
Illustrations by Sandy Magee
Cartoons by Randy Glasbergen
Book Design by Fiona Raven

First Printing 2011
Printed in Canada by Friesens

kaire.hughculver.com

For corporate inquiries and bulk orders,
please contact info@hughculver.com

For Dennis F. Culver

I'm sorry we couldn't share a laugh about this one.

And in the end,

it's not the years in your life that count.

It's the life in your years.

—ABRAHAM LINCOLN

Contents

Acknowledgements

When I jumped into this project, I assumed it would be a simple matter of typing some thoughts, getting an editor, and leaving the rest to some nameless professionals who would mysteriously get my first book onto bookshelves. Clearly, it doesn't work that way.

I am indebted to all the people from CAPS (Canadian Association of Professional Speakers) who responded to my calls for feedback. My hat is off to Roxanne Emmerich, who so brilliantly facilitated the CSP (Certified Speaking Professional) session in Orlando, put me on the hot seat, and got me to rethink not just the title of this book, but also the message. Many thanks to friends Daren Wride, Paul Hecht, and Nigel Brown, who read through some pretty horrible first drafts and gave honest feedback. Kudos to Michelle Kooistra for her attention to detail after an impressive overnight review. And a big nod to my friend Sandy Magee for sharing his artistic talent on this project.

A huge thanks to Fiona Raven, who took a word document and made it more than just presentable, and never once said it was 'good enough'. My sister Diana Alfred, bailed me out at the final stages with numerous heroic overnight proofreading episodes (was a comma needed in this sentence?). Who would have known that, after hiring editors in France, New York, and England, the best expertise was in my family?

And I bow down to my wife, Kirsten, and my daughters, Kate and Claire, for enduring my occasional disappearing acts as I worked through the rewrites. I hope you know that this is as much for you as it is for me.

Part I

• • •

IT'S ABOUT TIME

Getting honest about what defines success

Honesty is such a lonely word.

—BILLY JOEL, musician

Does This Sound Familiar?

Watson, you see but you do not observe.

—SHERLOCK HOLMES, detective

You are exhausted. Despite your best efforts to cross tasks off your To-Do list, endless interruptions, a deluge of email, and drawn-out meetings have a grip on your day. By midday you feel like the contortionist trying to escape from a straightjacket; your efforts look impressive, but get you nowhere. The paper is piling up, your list just got longer, and it seems the hallway outside your office has become social-central.

Sound familiar? Welcome to the club.

People just like you come to my workshops every year—looking for solutions to their ongoing treadmill of conflicting deadlines, unfinished projects, disappointments, and frustrations.

I usually start every session with the same three questions:

1) "Do you usually have more work to do in a day than you have time for?" All the hands in the audience quickly shoot up.

2) "Do you frequently finish your day saying to yourself, 'The day is over and I have no idea where it went'?" Everyone groans in affirmation.

3) "In the past three months, have you tried any new way—however small—to reorganize your day, prioritize work differently, change your patterns, or manage your time better?" Now only a few hands go up.

And there lies the irony—most people know they have a time-management problem, yet few take the time to do anything about it.

If we don't change our patterns, our ineffective approaches to workload and distractions will keep repeating themselves. The work may change, but there is little improvement in the approach. It's like the old joke: What is the definition of insanity? Answer: Doing the same thing over and over again, expecting a new result.

Here's a better question: What is the definition of *sanity*? Answer: Doing things differently until you get the result you are looking for.

Eventually you may reach the point of work overload where you think, "Enough is enough! I don't want to work this hard anymore, and I need to do something about it." Do you need to manage your time better? Of course. But first, ask yourself this: Will just crossing more items off my list satisfy me, or do I want to *experience* my time differently?

Anthony is, by all accounts, a winner. Good paying job, lots of responsibility, a healthy family, and he likes his work—maybe a bit too much. "I rarely turn work off. I can't," he admitted to me in a phone conversation. "If I don't stay on top of everything, I will pay later." Just like millions of hard-working people everywhere, Anthony's dedication to his vocation will have a cost, and eventually something will give. It's not unreasonable to predict that his work will suffer and that possibly his health and even relationships will follow suit.

Following the strategies I'm presenting in this book, Anthony now practices specific disciplines to unlock himself from work *before* he arrives home. Perhaps for the first time in years, he is committing himself to his time *away* from work with the same dedication and vigor that he commits to his work-time. Instead of working to have more time, this is how you would *make time work for you.*

My guess is that *you* also want more sanity and more balance between work, with all of its allure and complications, and your personal life, with all of its richness. All of this is possible, but it's not going to happen by learning a few email tricks or how to shuffle paper faster.

> Once you make the decision, the universe conspires to make it happen.
>
> —R.W. EMERSON,
> philosopher and leader of the Transcendentalist movement

The approach I've taken in this book is based on my own experience of unfolding the layers of ineffectiveness that have plagued my working career for three decades. I have looked at the patterns, habits, systems (you'll hear a lot about systems), and beliefs that have conspired to frustrate my efforts to create success and to have the kind of life I desire.

Of course, I will be providing you with some tools and better ways to plan and manage the distractions and work volume, but I hope you will agree that this book isn't just about tips and techniques.

I want you to rethink your approach to time *itself* and from there, to rebuild your approach to work, leisure, and life. This journey is full of potential and (unfortunately for most) is fully optional. But it is possible. I know, because I've done it.

I am well aware that self-help authors usually make bold claims about how their lives have turned around due to their new-found insights. They boast of their wonderful lifestyles, numerous homes, snazzy cars, and frequent trips to luxurious islands where they inevitably are sipping from drinks with umbrellas . . .

. . . I'm not going to do that.

When I started writing this book, it quickly became a cathartic experience of self-reflection. With every chapter, I found myself asking, "Am *I* really doing this?" It was painful to be promoting a formula for success while, in my own estimation, *still falling short*. Despite this, I continued to put these ideas on paper because I realize that perfection isn't my goal.

I don't work in a factory where work processes and tasks are repeated over and over; I live in a world that is constantly changing and challenging me to respond in the best possible way. And my guess is you live in that same world.

So, dear reader, I'm not predicting perfection, more wealth, or time sipping from drinks with umbrellas. But I am predicting that this book can provide something even better: growth.

If you use even one of the strategies in this book, you will grow in your ability to enjoy more success, have more free time, and get more of what you are looking for. That's what I *can* promise.

The solutions provided in this book are simple, and yet they work. I know this, because more than 3,000 people who have attended my live training sessions have experienced successful changes immediately. And because I use them myself, and they are still turning my life around for the better.

GETTING THE MOST FROM THIS BOOK

Being busy is a form of laziness—
lazy thinking and indiscriminate action.

—TIM FERRISS, author, serial entrepreneur
and ultra vagabond

Rest assured, these methods are simple to implement, and you won't have to purchase an expensive time-management system or new software. What you need to do—if you are committed to creating real change—is to:

1) Read this book.

2) Do the short exercises at the ends of the chapters.

3) Choose the solutions most relevant for you.

4) Practice those solutions for thirty days.

By the end of thirty days, your new habits will be formed. These habits will put you onto a path of change that will give you more time, more freedom, and more success.

If you are like me, you might get distracted somewhere in the third chapter with another book, or a new project, or some other life distraction. Don't. I'm going to suggest that you approach this book differently. I don't want you to read this book word for word—it's not necessary, nor is it a great use of your time.[1]

Instead, I want you to read this book more like a manual. Start with an overview (that's what this next section is about) and get an understanding of the *flow* of the book, so you know what to expect.

---

1.   I am sure some readers are quick readers, who read every word. But as 90% of the people who buy business books never finish them, I suggest there is both a reading and a motivation problem. See my side bar for how to double your reading speed.

Next, I encourage you to learn to read faster (see page 9). And whenever I provide an exercise, do it. These are going to help you to focus on what is important *for you*, to help you create real, lasting change. Your objective should be to find and pull out the concepts and skills that you need, not to plan for an exam.

OVERVIEW

Part I—"It's about Time" is about getting real about where time goes and how you are doing for time-efficiency. (Don't read these chapters alone—it's scary!) If you want to get to the heart of why you do what you do, pay particular attention to "Mirror, Mirror, on the Wall" (you'll thank me later).

Part II—"Systems" will give you the foundations for creating more time-success in all aspects of your work. This section is all about your systems: your planning, interruptions, meetings, email, and clutter. Be prepared—no sticky note, phone message, or wasted minute will be spared. Everything is under scrutiny (you *might* thank me later).

Part III—"Habits" is your toolbox for great habits (some of which you may have never thought of as habits). I want this to be a fun tour through options that are easy to apply, but that could have impressive long-term impact.

Part IV—"This is the Time" focuses on constant improvement and on keeping the flame lit. Getting the new System or Habit is only the start—the real benefit comes from practice.

Throughout the book, there are one-page worksheets. If you are anything like me, you will be tempted to skip these. Don't. It's important that you do some of the work of creating improvements as you read the book. I've kept it simple—take time for a little reflection, jot a few notes, make a few decisions. Your time commitment for each of these short exercises should be ten minutes or less.

I have also referenced some online resources that can be found at www.hughculver.com/breakbook. These are designed to support you as you practice your new strategies (feel free to share these with friends and colleagues).

Note: From time to time, I have inserted this symbol. Pay special attention to these thoughts and tips. These gems could make a big difference in the results you create.

Once and For All, How to Read

I took a speed-reading course and read 'War and Peace' in twenty minutes. It involves Russia.

–WOODY ALLEN, actor and playwright

How do you read a book? Are you a 'skimmer', flying through the pages, gleaning only what is valuable for you? Are you a 'starter'—slowly reading each word for the first five chapters and then losing interest or getting distracted with a new book? Simply based on statistics, I know it's unlikely you are a 'finisher'—few people are.

So I thought it would be helpful to give you some tips on how to get the most from this book. This is a simple approach, and certainly there are far more complicated approaches; but if you are a slow reader, you probably won't get through those, so here's a short version.

The average person reads at about 200–250 words per minute. With a few small improvements and a bit of practice, you should be able to double your reading speed and still have a comprehension rate of at least 75%. Here are some quick tips for reading faster and getting better retention and value out of books:

- **Plan to read.** You will have greater speed and retention if you read in a quiet place, at a time of day when you are fully awake, and when you have committed time to read.

- **Read the Table of Contents.** To get some idea of the flow of the book, take a couple of minutes and scan the list. The table of contents should also give you some idea of what parts of the book will have the most value for you, and what parts can be skimmed.

- **For each chapter, read the first paragraph,** then the subheads, and finally the last paragraph. Decide whether the chapter has any value for you. If not, move on to the next one.

- **Stop re-reading.** Use a device—a piece of paper, a ruler, or your finger—to move down the page, keeping your eye moving along with the device. Keep moving at a steady pace, slightly faster than comfortable.

- **Skip words.** You don't need to read every word to get sufficient comprehension. Start by reading the third or fourth word in from both ends of the line of text. This will prepare you to take "snapshots" of lines, rather than reading every word.

- **Create a goal.** You can quickly calculate your reading speed by averaging the number of words on a line and multiplying that number by the number of lines on the page. From there, it is easy to measure your speed for reading the page. Set a goal to double your reading speed. You will save time and probably not miss anything. For more tips on speed-reading, see www.hughculver.com/breakbook.

Ready to try your new skills? Here we go . . .

The Ultimate Currency

Running into the sun but I'm running behind.

—JACKSON BROWNE, "Running on empty"

Long before recorded history, we have been keeping track of time. The earliest examples were crude lunar calendars that predated the reforms of Julius Caesar's more exact Gregorian calendar by some 34,000 years. We've come a long way with recording time, and its importance in our everyday thinking and life has continued to increase. We use time as a measure of our day, as a record of our history, as a tool to compete against others, and as a way to find our location.

Think of time as the ultimate, universal, non-renewable currency. Virtually anywhere in the world, you can live a rich life by using it well, or you can squander it like a weekend gambler on a sortie to Las Vegas. High performers, who enjoy wonderful lives of wealth and personal freedom, have the same amount of time as the millions who are convinced that there is never enough time. Either way, once you use it, it is gone.

Whether we operate a stall in Marrakesh, teach primary school in Santiago, or arrive at our Seattle office by 9 am, time is democratic: we all get the same amount to start with. It's no different than the first cast of the die in a game of Monopoly. In life, every player gets the same amount of currency every time we wake up and pass 'GO': 24 hours; 1,440 minutes; 86,400 seconds.

What we do with time is always up to us, and that all starts with our perception.

As I have grown older, my perception of time has changed. When I was young, time seemed to go too slowly and I was restless for it to pass. In my twenties, I felt like I had all the time in the world and, for the most part, I enjoyed the luxury of designing my days as I wished. In my thirties, I learned to resent how other people could demand some of my time, and in my forties, I felt I had no time: work, schooling, family, and relationships filled every waking hour. I was busy perfecting "busy." Now, past the half-century mark, I truly regret time's passing—the lost opportunities and all the should-haves that I can't recapture. It's the same me—just a different perception of time.

Are You Satisfied?

There may be no 'i' in team, but there are two in 'idiot'.

There must be some reason why you have this book in your hand. Maybe you are already successful and are looking for an extra insight that will create even more success. Maybe you haven't achieved the success you want, and you want to learn how to better reach your goals. Or maybe you are frustrated with the way time slips through your fingers, and you want to change your habits but don't know how.

At a recent seminar that I was leading for university professors, a woman in the audience expressed exasperation about her workload and the impact on her family. She admitted she wasn't happy with some of her time habits.

"Every night I bring home my 'Guilt Bag'," she admitted. The woman explained that her Guilt Bag is her case, with laptop, notes, and files that need her attention.

When I asked her what she does with the bag once she arrives home, she described how she usually leaned it up against a wall and rarely worked on it. "And all night," she continued, "it stares at me, reminding me of my workload, and I feel more tired, anxious, and guilty." That's what I call negative programming—and it's all self-induced. It's also preventable.

For more than twelve years, I have been studying and teaching time management. I have probably read every current book on the subject, taken courses, written articles, interviewed masters, and spent endless hours working on my own performance. Here is the simple truth that I have discovered: *Time management is not the goal.*

In the end, nobody will care how we organize our minutes. *The only thing that will be measured is the value we create in the minutes we have.*

Before you read any further, I want you to ask yourself these three questions:

1) Do I start my day excited about what I am going to work on, and about what I am going to accomplish?

2) Do I usually finish my day smiling, with the feeling that comes from a day well spent?

3) Do I feel, for the most part, that I am in control of how I spend my time?

If you are reading this book with the ambition of becoming more time-effective, you will definitely learn some great skills and techniques for 'saving' time and getting more done in a day.[2]

But while becoming more effective at work is a laudable goal, it's not entirely why I wrote this book. I am interested in *how* you use your time, not in how much you can pack into your time. *Give Me a Break* is not only about better time management or about taking a physical break; it is also about developing a new outlook on how time can work *for* you.

Perhaps the best question to consider as you dive into this book and discover ways to reclaim more time in your day is: *What will you do with your new-found time?*

A LOOK IN THE MIRROR

If you fail to plan, you plan to fail.
–ANONYMOUS

Hyrum Smith, author of *The 10 Successful Laws of Time and Life Management* and modern pioneer of the day planner concept, discovered that most people have two self-limiting beliefs:

1) That someday we will have more time, and

2) That somehow we can save time.

Does this ring true for you? I certainly know that I lived with these same delusions for thirty years as I took my sloppy time-

---

2.   In our post-seminar surveys, we find that 95% of participants are saving at least one hour a day. This is time they can redirect to more important results in their work and life.

management habits with me, from business to business, from committee to committee, and into my personal life.

I was constantly dreaming up new projects and starting them before finishing the old ones. I could easily justify procrastination as a by-product of my ambitious nature, and multi-tasking was my badge of productivity. As I tried to accomplish three things at once, I did none of them well, and mostly ignored everyone around me.

Although I was rarely late for business meetings, I had a poor track record for picking up my daughters from school or piano lessons (twice I was actually on time, but at the wrong location). It seemed that I never had enough time and my appointments, meetings, and phone calls plagued my schedule and filled my To-Do lists.

My work and personal life were so out of balance that seven-day workweeks and sleeping at the office were not uncommon, nor were last-minute business trips to South America or cancelled dates with friends. I was frustrated. I knew I needed to change my patterns, but I didn't have a clue how to be successful and actually go home at a reasonable hour.

My ultimate excuse was that someday I would have more time for the pleasures of life. Just as Smith predicted, I believed that working faster than everyone else would save me time, but that mysterious bank of time never seemed to appear. I was oblivious to the evidence staring me in the face—that as I changed jobs, locations, and careers, the pattern simply traveled with me. Each time I found circumstances and people to blame (never me, of course!) for my woeful lack of work/life balance and high stress level.

Luckily, my condition wasn't permanent. Using the concepts and tools in this book, I eventually managed to create more success in my work, more balance with my family, and more satisfaction in my life.

So, how are you doing? Do you know where your time is being used well and where it isn't? Do you know which systems in your office are serving you and which are not? Do you really know the areas that you need to work on?

The first step in any development program or self-enlightenment program is always about awareness. You need to get very clear about the strengths that you want to keep and grow, and the areas of opportunity that are passing you by.

"My calendar is way overbooked and I'm three months behind in my work — *I don't have time to attend a time management seminar!*"

For years, I was delusional about my situation. I was convinced that I was working as hard as humanly possible.

Maybe I was, but I was a long way from working smart. It wasn't until I got clear about the cost my weaknesses were exacting on my business success, relationships, and health that I became serious about making change happen.

Self-assessment is the place to begin your path to a healthier relationship with time. The short quiz that follows mirrors the curriculum in this book and asks you to rate how well you are utilizing certain essential systems and habits.

I want you to take the quiz now, and again in thirty days.

In my seminars I call the first thirty days after the learning experience the "thirty-day challenge." This is the time it takes to create a new habit. It is also the time when you will either apply some of what you learned and benefit from it, or lose it.

The challenge is to see how much value you can get from those first thirty days.

Also, we need to repeat a new habit *with intent.* In other words, you have to really want the new habit to stick. Obviously you won't stick with a change in your diet, like from dairy to a diet of tofu and soy milk, if either one of these makes you nauseous. Similarly, adopting any strategies from this book won't stick if you don't have the intent to make them stick (or if they make you nauseous).

Take the quiz now. It should only take about three minutes to complete, and it will open your eyes to what needs to change.

If you are like me, you might be tempted to jump ahead to the next section. Don't do it. This quiz is an important starting point—it will help align the curriculum in this book with your specific needs. Go ahead and take the quiz now!

Time Management Self-Assessment Quiz

Based on a typical day, rate yourself against the following statements by circling one of the numbers (1=never, 2=rarely, 3=sometimes, 4=often, 5=always).

PRIORITIES

I start my day by reviewing what I will accomplish that day (high priority).	1	2	3	4	5
I avoid distractions and focus on what is most important, most of the time.	1	2	3	4	5
My goal is to accomplish priority tasks first, every day.	1	2	3	4	5
I plan my activities and priorities for the next day before leaving work.	1	2	3	4	5

GOALS

I have goals for the month or week.	1	2	3	4	5
I routinely set goals for all major projects or committee work.	1	2	3	4	5
My goals are visible and I constantly review them (at least weekly).	1	2	3	4	5
I constantly use my weekly goals to keep me on track and effective.	1	2	3	4	5

SYSTEMS

I have a time-management system that I use and keep updated.	1	2	3	4	5
My workspace is free of files, paper, sticky notes, etc.	1	2	3	4	5
I manage my email and other message volume well.	1	2	3	4	5
I try to match my work to my energy (e.g. hardest work in the morning).	1	2	3	4	5

HABITS

I am able to remove distractions and focus on the single task at hand.	1	2	3	4	5
When I find myself wasting time, I get back on track.	1	2	3	4	5
I manage my energy well and take regular health breaks every day.	1	2	3	4	5
When I leave work, I leave it behind.	1	2	3	4	5

CONSTANT IMPROVEMENT

I learn from others to improve my systems and habits.	1	2	3	4	5
I frequently review my habits and improve old habits that waste time.	1	2	3	4	5
In the last month, I have made an improvement to my time management.	1	2	3	4	5
I make time for education, relationships, and self-improvement.	1	2	3	4	5

OVERALL SCORE (Total each column and then get the sum of those 5 totals.)

To get a free copy of this quiz online, go to www.hughculver.com/breakbook.

As you review your scores for each of the five sections, here are some questions to consider:

HIGH SCORES (you rated yourself between 85 and 100): Look at the high scores you gave yourself. Why did you rate yourself high in those areas? What is the process or habit that supports that score? Often you can perform at a high level in some aspect of time management and not be aware that what you are doing is unique. Record at least one process or habit you are doing well that resulted in your high score.

....

....

MID-RANGE SCORES (you rated yourself between 70 and 85): Look for areas where you excel and have good performance. How can you reinforce these and support them always happening? Look at areas that you rated a '1', '2', or '3'—what is the pattern that is keeping you from scoring higher? Record at least one habit you have that resulted in the low score.

....

....

LOW SCORES (you rated yourself below 70): What are you doing that is inhibiting your performance? Think about your office set-up, your habits, your approach to creating and keeping goals. By becoming more aware of your patterns, you will be more able to create the change you need. List three of the most obvious areas in need of improvement (here are some examples):

- I know I procrastinate about the hardest goals.

- I don't start my day with a plan and by mid-morning I feel out of control.

- I have all the papers on my desk in neat piles, but they constantly distract me. I know I need to do something about it, but I don't want to forget anything.

- People drop by my desk all day. I don't want to be rude, but it makes it difficult to focus and get any work done.

I want to change/improve ....

....

I want to change/improve ....

....

I want to change/improve ....

....

Keep these areas of development in mind. The more focused you are on what you want to change, the more likely you are to find the solution in this book.

Where Does the Time Go?

Take care in your minutes,
and the hours will take care of themselves.
−LORD CHESTERFIELD, ambassador to Spain

"The day is over and I have no idea where the time went!"

Do you ever wonder where the time goes? For many people, the day is a blur of meetings, phone calls, interruptions, email, and last-minute problems that need to be dealt with right now.

With all of our clients, the same three distractions always seem to be at the scene of the crime:

1) Email

2) Interruptions

3) Meetings

We call these the "Big Three Time Thieves" and they are the rust that eats away at performance and seems to grow incessantly. Here's a quick rundown on them:

Email—Most people have no idea how much time they actually are spending on email. It can become one long stream of lost minutes between morning scans while commuting (not while driving, obviously!), a constant bombardment while at your desk, quick peeks during meetings, in elevators, waiting in line at Starbucks, or at the ball park while pretending to watch your child chewing gum in left field.

One Microsoft survey found that employees were spending, on average, one hour and forty-five minutes a day on email (note that this means some people are spending much more time than this). My guess is that, for many of us, we spend twice that amount of time.

The ubiquitous nature of email (on your computer at work, your laptop at home, your smart phone in your car, etc.) means that it can become a normal part of the day, like breathing and walking, that fills most of your available moments.

Is it really necessary to be that available? Certainly we used to survive admirably with only phones, faxes, and meetings. Common sense would suggest (and if it doesn't, I will) that there is a downside to being always connected and constantly checking who has sent you something on your phone. But as Will Rogers once quipped, "Just because something is common sense, doesn't mean it is common."

Interruptions—Interruptions can eat up your day. Just think of the people who drop by to chat, the non-urgent phone calls, the interruptions from vendors with their latest pitches, and distracting office noise. Workshop participants typically tell me that they have to deal with at least one hour of interruptions a day.

What percentage of your day is lost due to low-value interruptions that could be diverted to someone else, dealt with faster, or avoided altogether?

Meetings—If you are in meetings just one hour per day (many of our clients report that meetings typically eat up about three hours of their day), and you work 250 days per year, more than thirty-one of those days are spent in meetings over the course of a year. What percentage of this time is really necessary, and what percentage is being chewed up in poor-quality or unnecessary meetings?

As part of your look in the mirror, let's put some numbers together to show how your time is being spent. Below you will find a table designed to help you calculate where your time goes. In the example on the left-hand side, I have inserted average time spent per day by our clients on the Big Three (email, interruptions, and meetings): 1.75 hours on email, 1 hour on interruptions, and 1 hour in meetings. Calculated over 250 working days in a year, this adds up to twenty-three work-weeks (based on a forty-hour work week) per year.[3]

Do I have your attention now?

In a nutshell, you spend about one-half of your working years on email, interruptions, and meetings.

Now try it for yourself: do the calculation in the following chart (using the formula provided).

---

3.   Allowing for an average of a one-day holiday per month, there are about 250 working days in a year.

Annual Time Used on the Big Three

TYPICAL AMOUNT OF TIME USED			YOUR AMOUNT OF TIME USED		
The Big Three	Calculation	Work-weeks per year	The Big Three	Calculation	Work-weeks per year
Email	(1.75 hrs. × 250 days) /40 hrs.	11	Email	(____ hrs. × 250 days) /40 hrs.	
Interruptions	(1 hr. × 250 days) /40 hrs.	6	Interruptions	(____ hrs. × 250 days) /40 hrs.	
Meetings	(1 hr. × 250 days) /40 hrs.	6	Meetings	(____ hrs. × 250 days) /40 hrs.	
Total time		23 weeks	Total time		

Were you surprised by the total? Most people don't think in terms of week after week of time losses, and certainly not in terms of a full year. But if you are going to value your time more and be committed to making the small changes every day, this is exactly the perspective you need to take.

Now imagine being able to get back even five percent of that lost time. That alone, over the course of a year, could be as much as a whole work-week. In fact, here is a great formula to remember:

Ten minutes a day saved is equivalent to about one week per year of recovered time that you can redirect to more important work, to planning, to relationship-building, or to growing your business.[4]

Ten minutes per day = One week per year

---

4.   This is a rough calculation that obviously depends on the hours you work in a year. 10 min/day × 250 days/year = 2,500 minutes. 2,500 min/60 = 41.6 hours, or about one forty-hour work-week.

This is the power of making small changes consistently every day to maximize your use of time. It's no different from putting deposits in your bank, starting an exercise routine, or improving your diet. Initially you can feel discouraged because the results aren't visible, but over time the small improvements become big payoffs you can enjoy.

And now I'm going to show you how . . .

A Model for Change

*Opportunity is missed by most people because
it is dressed in overalls and looks like work.*

–THOMAS EDISON, inventor extraordinaire

I f you don't get your work done today, you will have it tomorrow. The pile of unfinished work will accumulate, and with it will come frustration, anxiety, and stress. So you have two choices: work harder (which most of us try to do already) or work smarter.

In school we learned about cell biology, dividing exponential numbers, and conjugating verbs. Unfortunately, our sixth grade teacher didn't provide us with more practical life lessons, like how to prioritize.

Rarely at school were we asked to decide what was the most important work. Instead, we were rewarded for getting everything on our list done, without exception.

Once the responsibilities and workloads build up to the point where you know you can't get it all done, this approach doesn't work anymore. You are left knowing that mitochondria has something to do with ATP, but no clue what to do with your ever-growing To-Do list.

What you need is a new way of looking at your workload, and a new approach for moving from overwhelm to getting work done. Unfortunately, this won't happen just because you buy a new day planner or learn a few tricks on your BlackBerry. And while most well-meaning time management training programs are about making you more efficient at processing work faster, I doubt that this is your aspiration.

Beware the Downward Slide

Just as water always prefers to flow downhill, we typically migrate to what is easier in life. Maybe your habit is to put off making sales calls, or coaching that recalcitrant, underperforming salesperson, until you have spent the morning reviewing emails. Or maybe a project you committed to hasn't gotten off the ground because of minor interruptions and general busy-ness.

That pattern won't change by learning a little trick for sending emails faster. It requires a more wholesale change, and that starts with your beliefs and the mental pattern of prioritization that you have established over time.

Darren, a manager at a large insurance company, is responsible for thirteen insurance adjusters. He has many responsibilities, including training new staff, coaching existing staff, and conducting performance reviews. His time-management style was what I call the Radar Approach—when something came into view, he treated it with the same priority as everything else, regardless of its real value, who sent it, or how old it was.

The Radar Approach is a chaotic way to manage workload, because you are constantly chasing after the newest interruption and leaving behind what you are already working on. No doubt Darren was achieving some success with this approach, but the problem was that nothing long-term was being addressed. Darren's workdays were full of frenetic, 'put-out-fires' experiences that left him exhausted and frustrated.

Without a new system, he was destined to repeat this frustrating pattern over and over again.

Sound familiar?

Coming Full Circle

The model I am going to show you is what Darren and hundreds of our clients are using to get a fresh start on their patterns and to create dramatic improvements in their results. First, I will give you a quick overview of the five parts of the model—Beliefs, Goals, Systems, Habits, and Continuous Improvement. Then, in the remainder of the book, I will provide more detail about each part, starting with the chapter, "Mirror, Mirror, on the Wall."

Confession time: I know that every time-management book worth its salt has a model. Some models are about the three ways, seven habits, 101 secrets, etc. I realize that, by introducing *my* model, I'm following a predictable path. Please bear with me. This simple model is just to provide some glue to the sections in the book. The real heart of the book is found in the individual parts: Beliefs, Goals, Systems, Habits, and Continuous Improvement.

Beliefs

After awareness, when we recognize an opportunity to improve, we have to always revisit our beliefs. It is our belief about our ability to create change that is the pivotal point for changing results. Negative, self-defeating beliefs such as: "There is only so much I can get done in a day," or "Interruptions make it impossible for me to concentrate and complete my work," will stymie our best efforts to get work done effectively or to improve.

You need to believe that you are the master of your time, and not the victim of other people's agendas. Remember that you will always get more of what you focus on—this is never truer than with time management. If you think you are swamped by your workload and will never get caught up, guess what? You won't! And if you think other people's agendas are constantly interfering with your ability to get work done, guess what? They are! Just as Henry Ford famously forewarned, "Whether you think you are right or you think you are wrong, you are probably right!"

If, instead, you think that you are capable of finding time to get organized and to work on priorities, guess what? Opportunities will show up for moving forward on your biggest goals. By switching your focus from what *you can't do* to what *you can do*, you open up a world of possibilities.

Sound like simplistic, positive-thinking mumbo jumbo? Maybe so, but it works. In the chapter, "Mirror, Mirror, on the Wall," I am going to challenge you to really look at what you believe about time, and to recreate those beliefs so that they serve you, every day.

Goals

Our client research has discovered an alarming fact: people don't make personal goals. Of course, they probably have a plan for their business, their marketing strategy, or their product launch, *but they don't use the one thing that will generate the biggest results: personal goals.*

In a post-program study of participants in our program, we found that those participants who began a new habit of setting goals at the end of each day and of planning the next day's schedule had by far the most dramatic increases in time-management success (by the way, I define success as feeling satisfied with how my time was spent).

The "Goals Work" chapter will give you a simple formula for goal setting, and the "Plan like a Pilot" chapter will show you how to create your Action Plan for the week—this is easily the best improvement you can make to your time-management thinking and results.

Systems

Systems are great sources of efficiency and productivity (think filing systems, phone systems, or bookkeeping systems). When you lack good systems, you are destined to forever repeat your time-wasting behavior. For example, if you don't have a good paper management system, you will always be frustrated by clutter on your desk. And lack of a system for email means time wasted re-reading emails, dealing with unwanted messages, and manually sorting your Inbox.

The good news is that small changes in your systems can create enormous time savings. For example, if you could save just ten minutes every day by starting meetings on time and having a well-designed agenda, you could free up an entire work-week every year.

Habits

More than 300 years ago, Samuel Johnson accurately described the incredible influence of habits when he said, "The chains of habits are too weak to be felt until they are too strong to be broken." When you improve a habit (how you plan your week, start your mornings, or how you tackle big projects), your new habit automatically, and with little effort, starts working for you. It's like finding that perfect investment—once you see the opportunity and make the investment, it will start working for you.

Continuous Improvement

Be honest: what have you done in the last month to improve your time-management success? If you are anything like most participants in our training programs, the answer is *nada*.

In our seminars, 80–90% of participants have never taken a course or spent more than one hour learning how to use Microsoft Outlook—yet most of them are using it every day!

Most haven't changed their office layout in years, are always rushed in the morning (and don't know why), use the same excuses to explain their procrastination, and allow the same people to interrupt them all day.

One of the best ways to improve your success is to continually renew and improve. By asking yourself what is working and what could be improved, you will start to see opportunities for improvement. Having this attitude of continuous improvement will make work more interesting, provide you with more freedom, and bring you more success—every day.

I'm glad we have gotten the one and only model in the book out of the way. Now it's time to get to the biggest source for change: what you say to yourself.

Mirror, Mirror, on the Wall

*It's easier to say 'No'
when there is a deeper 'Yes' burning inside.*

—STEPHEN R. COVEY, international best-selling author

M ost of our challenges are self-created because of our self-limiting beliefs. And the same applies to our frustrations with time. Our beliefs got us into the time management challenges we are experiencing, and our beliefs will get us out.

As Pogo, Walt Kelly's famous 1960s comic strip character, famously exclaimed, "We have met the enemy and he is us."

Your belief about your ability to get work completed, and your belief about your ability to change your

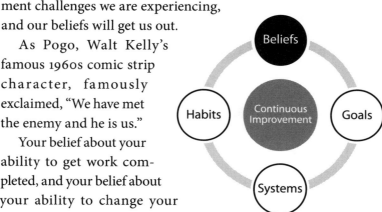

patterns, will be either the lock or the key to creating more success. It's as simple as that—and as hard as that: all significant changes in our lives begin by changing our beliefs. The challenge is that the ones that don't serve us are invisible, working in the background to sabotage our efforts, and are frustratingly difficult to reverse.

"When we learn a bad habit, it takes over the brain map in that area," explains Norman Doidge, M.D. in his remarkable book, *The Brain That Changes Itself.* "This is why it is so hard to 'unlearn' a bad habit. It has residency first, like an unwanted roommate."

When I was in the tourism industry, my belief was that I needed to keep my schedule open every day to see what would happen. I operated from a simple To-Do list that seemed to have a life of its own as it grew longer daily. My days were packed with phone-call interruptions, friends dropping in (our office was in a public marketplace in Vancouver), impromptu meetings, and conversations with customers and staff. It was chaotic, but I had no idea that I was the architect of the chaos. In fact, I became a pro at blaming my frustrations on others and on my environment.

I was convinced that successful people must be really good at handling crisis. My logic was simple: I was successful and surrounded by chaos; therefore people more successful must just be better at dealing with chaos.

What I failed to pay attention to were the successful business leaders who were also extremely efficient. You know—the leaders with uncluttered desks, meticulous planning, and measured habits developed over years of trial and error. I assumed that *those* leaders must have other people doing all the work for them.

Beliefs, Beliefs, Beliefs

Only now do I recognize that, by believing chaos was a normal, I actually allowed it to happen. In short, I was putting my energy into convincing myself that I was doing my best instead of looking for *how I could improve.*

Until I changed what I believed, I was destined to operate from crisis—in that business and in every enterprise I created. This led to a stressful pattern of desperate, last-minute efforts to meet deadlines, and missed opportunities. The more I justified my belief with evidence, the more entrenched I became in my ineffective approach.

Here's a simple formula that applies to literally all aspects of your life. It is the secret to why you experience success in certain areas of your life—like a relationship, or your education, or your ability to earn money—and it is the exact cause of where you fail.

- ✓ *First, we make up our beliefs. Rightly or wrongly, we are the author of our stories.*

- ✓ *Second, we forget we made them up. Yep! We believe what we believe, and we love to be right.*

- ✓ *Next, we act as if the belief is true. Ever been convinced you were in the right, despite pretty strong evidence to the contrary (like arriving home late for dinner because you decided to work "just a few more minutes" at the office)?*

- ✓ *And finally, we look for evidence to prove we are right. That's right—if you think that co-worker is an idiot, guess what you will notice?*

Here's a quick exercise to prove to you the incredible influence of your beliefs.

To make this exercise most effective, you need to hold a piece of paper over the right-hand column of figures. Please do that now.

As I ask you each question, try to answer it, and then slide the paper down just enough to reveal the correct answer in the right-hand column.

Let's try it with the first example.

If the following image is a Roman numeral, how do you add a single line to make it a six?

Okay, you got that one right. Do a happy dance and now go to the next one . . .

And, if the following image is a Roman numeral, how do you add a single line to make it a seven?

Again, slide your paper down to reveal the answer.

(answer below)

And, if the following image is a Roman numeral, how do you add a single line to make it an eight?

Again, slide your paper down to reveal the answer.

(answer below)

Okay, you are on a roll! Now, in the following image, how do you add a single line to make it a six?

When you are ready, slide your paper down to reveal the answer.

(answer below)

If you are like virtually everyone who takes this exercise (assuming you didn't peek), you got stumped at the fourth iteration. Your brain couldn't come up with a solution for adding a single line to make "ɪx" into six. But wait!

Are you looking at the problem from an *objective* point of view, unobscured by history or beliefs you might have conjured up based on the previous instructions? Or are you looking at it *through your belief window* and spending more time looking for evidence to prove that you are right ("I knew it, there is no solution for making this Roman numeral into a six with only one line!") instead of thinking creatively?

Notice that I didn't tell you that the last example was Roman numerals but, because the first three examples were about Roman numerals, almost everyone makes the assumption that the last one would be as well.

The reality is that, if you were presented with the last iteration of this problem first: "How do you add a single line to 'ɪx' to make it 'sɪx'," I think you would quickly arrive at the correct answer—that you just need to add an 's' to 'ɪx' to make 'sɪx'.

Let's go through what I think happened here:

First, you were given enough evidence to create a belief that you were working with Roman numerals, *and* you were successful in creating the right answers. This combination of a belief and a confirmation that the belief was correct, was repeated enough times to make it reliable.

Next, you were provided with quite a different challenge, but your belief that this was all about Roman numerals inhibited your willingness to examine the problem more closely, and you got stuck.

Your new belief (which was created in a matter of moments) tells you that you are good at Roman numerals, but this last puzzle is a tough one. You think, maybe it can't be solved? Or it's a trick question. But in fact, the answer is so incredibly simple that a six year-old could probably solve it (if that was the only problem they were given to solve).

As an adult, we love being right and, once we create a belief, we go to work to prove that it is a correct one.

What beliefs do you have that prevent you from creating more success? Maybe, for example, you believe:

- You work better under pressure.

- Nothing can improve until your boss changes her or his ways.

- The nature of your job is to blame for the long hours you work.

- No one can prepare a quotation/letter/proposal/agenda as well as you can.

Certainly, in the tourism industry we always had the ultimate excuse—the time of year. I can remember trying to get staff to plan ahead and to work more from goals. But between May and September, the excuse was that there was too much going on to revisit our goals and adjust our strategies. In the slow season, I would again try to rally the troops to get organized and look at goals, but by then the excuse was that they didn't have the energy for it. So we would repeat this cycle of feast to famine and never really get ahead of the game with our planning.

Let's take a look at some old beliefs (maybe they will look familiar), and how to rewrite them to better advantage.

Old Belief, New Belief—It's Your Choice

For each 'old belief' I present, ask yourself if it sounds at all familiar, and then ask yourself if it still serves you. Be honest with yourself. The first (and hardest) step in all change is awareness; we have to be honest about what is holding us back from making changes.

Okay, here we go. I'm going to present just five dysfunctional beliefs and some better alternatives. You will probably be able to add to this list with ones of your own. If so, let me know!

1) Old Belief: "I've done pretty well so far, so why change?"

Yes, you probably do have some approaches to time management that work for you. For example, many of the people who have taken our course are already well-organized when it comes to preparing for and attending meetings. On the other hand, after they leave the meetings, they procrastinate on what they committed to.

> *"I was going to buy a copy of The Power of Positive Thinking, and then I thought: 'What the hell good would that do?'"*
> —RONNIE SHAKES, comedian

Better Belief: "I know that better is always possible and I am looking forward to earning more freedom with my time."

2) Old Belief: "I work best under pressure."

This is a classic belief, and one that I embraced for many years. When we learn that we are good under pressure, and in fact get rewarded for it, it's inevitable that our success will depend on last-minute rushing. This belief can lead to procrastination, unnecessary crises, and frustration with others on your team.

Better Belief: "I enjoy working from a plan, crossing tasks off my list, and having less stress."

3) Old Belief: "It's impossible to plan for my day. I have to be able to respond to the chaos around here."

This is a hugely popular belief for people who work in customer-service roles, such as front counters in banks, hotels and recreation centers, or deep in the IT and administrative departments of many companies. The reality is that if you don't plan, you will constantly be frustrated by interruptions, and these interruptions will emerge as part of your self-fulfilling prophecy.

Better Belief: "With a plan I can keep long-term projects moving forward."

4) Old Belief: "I don't have a good track record for keeping promises to myself."

It is true that most people have a hard time keeping promises to themselves. I read once that only 12% of people keep their New Year's resolutions. Don't be too hard on yourself—it is possible that you aren't paying attention to successes you have created. Do you show up for work on time? Do you obey traffic laws? You are already a promise-keeper. You just need to get into a habit of creating even more goals, and committing to completing them.

Better Belief: "I am a promise-keeper and I am strengthening that skill every day."

5) Old Belief: "I have tried time-management systems in the past and I never stick with them for more than a week."

Okay, I have to admit I am also one of those people who have taken time-management courses and only stuck with the plan for a short while. Here's the problem with many time-management courses: they take too much time! There are special pages to be completed each day, review charts to fill out, and percentages-of-an-hour to be calculated. Within a week, you are spending more time filling in your Day-Timer than you are spending getting work done. What you need is a process for being more effective that seems effortless to execute. Don't worry: that's what this book is about.

Better Belief: "With a simple system I can manage my time better and still have flexibility for what comes up."

New beliefs are not created by positive thinking. The brain will never be fooled by your attempts to change years of patterned thinking by just chanting a new mantra. The synapse pathways are too entrenched and the knee-jerk reactions too engrained.

What is needed is a combination of the new belief married with some tangible evidence. In other words, prove to your brain that the belief works, and you are well on your way to creating a new pathway.

A Formula for Success

When I used to race whitewater kayaks, I had to learn how to maneuver my wafer-thin racing boat around hanging poles (called 'gates') as fast as possible, while negotiating through some pretty wild whitewater. If you make one small mistake, the river's current will blow you past the gate and you are penalized.

It was easy to be intimidated by the power of the river, and the ruthless way it discarded paddlers who missed critical strokes, and flushed them downstream. I can remember standing on the river shore, watching paddlers struggling to stay upright and hold their course, and noticing my own doubts surfacing.

The trick I learned was to be aware of what was happening and to change my belief quickly. Watching other paddlers struggle was making me doubt my own abilities (not a good thing), and weakening my resolve for when it would be my turn (really not a good thing).

Next, I had to remind myself of my training and all the days I had spent on rivers wilder than this one. And then the critical last step was to really pay attention to little successes I enjoyed when I was in my boat. I nailed that turn; I powered over to number four gate and got through clean; I made the spin and backed through number five clean.

With every success, I reinforced my belief in my abilities; I was adding evidence to the belief.

On race day, my belief was entrenched and ready to serve me. Small setbacks were overlooked because of the strength of my belief in my abilities. In effect, this is exactly how we create successful change in our life:

1) Become crystal clear about the challenge,

2) Determine the best possible solution,

3) Adopt a belief that you will succeed,

4) Take action and pay attention to evidence of your success, and

5) Repeat.

Let's look at a simple formula to represent this process: adopt a new belief, prove it works, and repeat.

$$(\text{New Belief} + \text{Evidence}) \times \text{Repeat} = \text{New Success}$$

Here is another great example: I used to believe that I worked better under pressure (see Old Belief #2, above). This helped me to get a lot done, and to get it done faster than most people I knew.

The problem was, I was looking at the wrong evidence. While I was focusing on what a hero I was for doing all-nighters and accomplishing incredible amounts of work, I was ignoring how

"Before we begin our Time Management Seminar, did everyone get one of these 36-hour wrist watches?"

disastrous my life was in other areas. My lack of planning meant that I was constantly going from unproductive to overwhelmed. There was no steady state and I was ignoring the important, but not urgent, leadership work of building successful relationships and planning.

My new belief is that I love the feeling of working from a plan and having less stress. The evidence I focus on is the clarity and productivity I enjoy at work, and being able to go home at a reasonable hour. I also notice that short periods of 'unproductive' time (going for a walk, reading, meeting with a friend) in the day can reward me with a sense of calm and better attention for when I am re-engaged. The more I focus on evidence that working from my plan is paying big dividends, the more entrenched and useful my belief becomes.

(New Belief + Evidence) × Repeat = New Success

Think about your own beliefs—which ones serve you well and which ones do you need to change?

Once you have defined the new belief, start to look for evidence that supports it. Is your new belief that you can be satisfied with 'good quality' work (as opposed to seeking perfection)? Or maybe that other people can—and should—have more ownership over work that you have controlled in the past? Great!

Now notice any evidence that this new belief is serving you. Maybe you notice that the meeting agenda you had someone else prepare (for a change) was actually quite good. And notice that you saved yourself twenty minutes of tedious work putting the agenda together.

The next time the same task comes up, revisit your evidence and remind yourself of your new belief. Just like a river carving a new path, the more it runs its course, the more entrenched and permanent the path becomes.

Now, it is time to put it on paper . . .

Beliefs Worksheet

As you were reading the list of beliefs above, you might have recognized one you have that no longer serves you. (Example: "It's impossible to plan for my day. I have to be able to respond to the chaos around here.") Write that belief in the space provided below.

My old belief:

....

....

Now create a replacement belief that will serve you better. (Example: "When I start the day with a plan and stick to it, I enjoy more success and less stress.") Write this new belief in the present tense, as if it were true today.

My new belief:

....

....

What evidence proves this new belief to be true? In other words, what proof do you have that this new belief will work for you? If your new belief is, "Once I put my plan on paper, I can let work go and not think about it until tomorrow," what is the evidence to support it? (Example: "I enjoyed a relaxing evening with the kids and felt more rested when I returned to work.")

Evidence to support my new belief:

....

....

Finally, you need to post your new belief where you can see it often. Repeat this goal to yourself every morning and anchor it in your subconscious. Remember, this process is going to rewire years of programming—day after day, with each repeat, the magic starts to happen.

(New Belief + Evidence) × Repeat = New Success

Getting Your Boulders Rolling

If you have to swallow two frogs,
swallow the big one first, and don't look at it too long.

—MARK TWAIN, author and humorist

One of the simplest and yet most remarkable economic theories comes from a nineteenth-century Italian economist named Vilfredo Pareto. When studying the wealth distribution in northern Italian villages, Pareto discovered that about 80% of the wealth was held by about 20% of the citizens. In every community he studied, a similar ratio of wealth distribution appeared.

This magic ratio is now commonly referred to as the 80/20 Rule, or Pareto's Principle. The 80/20 Rule can also be stated as, "Eighty percent of the results you get in life come from only 20% of your activities." The depressing flipside is that about 80% of our activities only lead to about 20% of our desired results.

Does this ring true for you? Think about all the activities that occupy your day—which ones actually make the most difference to your success? If you are involved in sales, the three sales calls you made this morning were far more valuable than the four hours of interruptions, reading emails, and meetings that followed.

If you are a manager, you might invest thirty minutes to coach an employee, and it could improve that person's results for months to come. On the other hand, the same thirty minutes spent repairing their mistakes only produces a short-term benefit.

Beliefs

Habits

Continuous Improvement

Goals

Systems

So the secret to success—in business and in life—is to spend as much time as possible working on the 20% of activities that create 80% of the results. To do this, you first have to be able to distinguish high-value activities from low-value activities, and to get better at working on the former while avoiding the latter.

Okay, I know this much should be obvious, but now I want to show you how to re-frame, to make it easier to stay focused on what is important. To do this, we will use new definitions for all the activities that fill your day: **Boulders, Pebbles, and Sand.**

Boulders

Boulders are your long-term goals. These are the high Return-On-Investment (ROI) objectives that give you the best results. Boulders are not completed in one day, and are usually the hardest to find time to complete.

Examples of Boulders are:

- Executing a plan with your team

- Marketing to a new territory

- Building or revamping a website

- Purchasing new equipment

- Launching a new sales campaign

- Improving an internal system (bookkeeping, invoicing, etc.)

- Designing a new brochure

- Staff development (hiring, training, etc.)

Pebbles

Then we have Pebbles. Pebbles are tasks; the productive kind of work that occupies your day. Pebbles can be single, stand-alone tasks, such as preparing a quote for a client, or they can be chunks  of a Boulder, such as organizing a meeting for a project committee or getting quotes for equipment purchases. Pebbles can usually be completed in one day, one meeting, one phone call, or one visit. When you are working on your Pebbles, you are working on the 20% that gets you 80% of your results.

Examples of Pebbles are:

- Drafting a proposal

- Calling vendors for quotations

- Writing new sales copy for your website

- Updating your calendar for sales milestones

- Making sales calls

- Coaching staff

- Following up on a client enquiry

- Taking a course on using email

Sand

Finally, there is Sand. Sand is the least productive use of your time. Time spent on Sand has few rewards and is part of the 80% of your time that only pro-duces 20% of your results.

Examples of Sand are:

- Much of your email

- Micromanaging other people's work

- Unnecessary interruptions

- Reading about issues you have little influence over

- Scanning reports not relevant to your work

- Surfing the Internet

- Attending poorly planned meetings

- Spending time in irrelevant conversations

These tasks seem especially designed to get your attention and steal your time. The overall goal of *Give Me a Break* is to show you how to work at completing your **Pebbles**, so you can accomplish all of your **Boulders** while staying out of the **Sandbox**.

The Boulders, Pebbles, Sand Demonstration

One day, a professor placed a large glass pitcher in front of his class, and instructed the students to think of the vessel as representing the time they have in the day. "If you work from 8:30 am until 4:30 pm, then that is what the vessel represents," he said. "Whatever you can fit into the vessel gets completed. And what does not fit is left over for you to face the next day."

Next, the professor proceeded to put large boulders into the vessel. One after another, he placed them on top of each other. "These are your projects," he explained. "When you start your day, you want to focus on these and work on them as soon as possible."

Then he produced a bag of small pebbles, and these he added to the vessel. Each pebble slipped through the cracks between the boulders to fill the spaces. "Now I am adding all the important tasks and steps you need to take during your day to accomplish your work."

Finally, he poured a small amount of sand into the vessel. Some of the sand filtered through the pebbles and boulders to the bottom. Some filled the space in between. "And finally, we have sand," he explained. "Sand represents the low-value interruptions in your day that distract you from your real work. It's inevitable that you will have sand. Your objective is to minimize its influence on your productivity."

"What lesson can you take from this demonstration?" he asked the students.

"That sand is inevitable?" suggested one student.

"Yes, that is true, but that's not the only point of this demonstration," the professor replied.

"The point I want you to take away," he continued, "is that when you start with your boulders, you assure that the most important work is getting done, despite the distractions."

With that, the professor reached under the desk and produced a can of beer. Pulling the tab, and with great ceremony and a smile, he poured the beer into the vessel and announced to the class, "And remember, when all is done, there is always room for a beer!"

A Useful Language

Here is a neat side benefit to thinking in terms of *Boulders, Pebbles, and Sand*—it is a valuable re-frame for your staff and team, and a helpful way to get everyone on the same page quickly.

After attending my seminar, a vice-president client of ours decided to put Boulders, Pebbles, and Sand into action. Gathering her immediate team in her office, she wrote, "Boulders" at the top of a white board. "For the next twenty minutes, I had the team share the Boulders that they were working on, while I listed them," she recalled. "What was amazing was how many boulders were being addressed, and how many weren't priorities in my mind. Clearly we were getting lost in a sea of goals, objectives, priorities, and miscellaneous targets."

Next, she and her team reduced their list to the most important Boulders, and refocused their activities to align with the new list. "From now on," she said, "we use the word 'Boulders' to galvanize the team toward the most important priorities. With everyone so busy in their own departments, it's a simple shift, but a critical one."

A Quick Definition

Sometimes people get confused about the definitions of **Boulders, Pebbles, and Sand.** Here are quick definitions that can help:

Boulders are long-term goals—projects, purchases, new hires, strategic initiatives, etc. Boulders usually take many weeks, and many steps, to complete. And these are the most important to keep moving forward.

Pebbles are tasks—phone calls, meetings, reports, etc., that are valuable. Some may be independent and stand-alone tasks, like calling a supplier or coaching an employee. Often your pebbles are connected to the completion of a Boulder. Pebbles can usually be completed in one sitting, one conversation, one meeting, etc.

Sand represents low-value interruptions—people dropping by your desk to chat, some phone calls, much of your email, etc. Sand often looks important—"Hey, have you got a minute?"—but it typically fails to produce a meaningful result.

I hope that helps! For more information and tips to help keep your Boulders rolling, and to stay out of the Sandbox, go to www.hughculver.com/breakbook.

The Pareto Principle Goes to Work

If you are like most people who work at a desk, you come in to the office, grab a coffee, sit down at your computer, and go to work on your email. By mid-morning, you're feeling pretty good about your progress. You had fifty-five new emails when you came in, and now you have replied to eighteen, deleted twelve, and have twenty-five more to go. Three people have dropped by your desk to chat about the weekend or to ask you a question. You have answered the phone five times, but none of the calls were about client work. The tasks that typically fill your morning hours involve email, phone calls, and interruptions.

Thinking about the Pareto Principle, you have just spent your morning working on the 80% of the tasks that create the least value for you. To be blunt: you have spent the morning in the Sandbox.

Of course, some of the email conversations have value, but mostly your activities are driven by other people's agendas, not yours.

> *There cannot be a crisis next week, my schedule is already filled.*
>
> —HENRY KISSENGER, political scientist and diplomat

By mid-morning, your stress level has risen, you are frustrated, and any plan you might have created is out the window. You are fully in reaction mode.

Don't get me wrong—if you are an air traffic controller or a front-desk receptionist, you probably should be leaving your time open to respond to what comes your way. However, my experience is that 99% of us want to, *and can*, work differently.

The solution is to always start your day working from a plan that points the majority of your activity toward completing your Boulders. Of course you will have needless interruptions and unwanted email—we all do. But when you are proactive in your planning, and diligent in choosing which interruptions to spend time on, your results dramatically improve.

*   *   *

Shelly is a recreation programmer for a municipal government. Her job is to develop, market, and deliver fitness, education, sports, and other leisure options for local residents. Her planning deadlines are critical, and yet interruptions, distractions, and new objectives make her job stressful.

"I know what I need to work on," she told me, "but I can't seem to find time in the day. Everything gets pushed to the last minute. It happens constantly, and I hate it." Sand has crept in and taken over Shelly's time, leaving little time for planning or for working on Pebbles and Boulders. Until she becomes proactive, by starting every day with a plan that is completely oriented toward her Boulders, Shelly's pattern of frustration will repeat itself.

So how successful are you at working on the 20% that makes the most difference? Do you even have your Boulders clearly defined? Is your plan for the day aligned with your Boulders? And how much Sand is creeping into your day, distracting you with false urgencies?

In the next section, I am going to challenge you to take the Time Audit. This is one of the most powerful, scary, and revealing exercises I have ever done. It completely changed my outlook on time, and I think it will do the same for you.

> Focus on Boulders. Complete Pebbles.
> Stay out of the Sandbox.

Getting Honest about Time

Few things are more powerful than holding a mirror to our own lives and taking a good, hard look. My first appointment with a financial advisor was a surprise that left an indelible impression on me, and changed my money-spending habits from that day forward. Rather than dole out the expected investment advice about mutual funds or dollar cost averaging, he suggested I record how I was currently spending my money.

For two weeks, I had to carefully record every purchase I made, from the large amounts for groceries and gas to the smaller amounts for magazines and coffee. It was painful. Every day, I dutifully recorded my financial impulses and discretions. And then came the day of reckoning—looking at my total expenses.

I suddenly realized how totally unaware I was of my spending habits—including my coffee-drinking habit.

The coffee for my morning commute, the break-time coffee, the post-lunch take-out, and that afternoon café latté were adding up. By the end of the two-week exercise, and after calculating my costs in pre-tax dollars, I realized I was working one and a half weeks a year for Starbucks!

I was so shocked by the lesson, and by my cavalier spending habits, that I resolved to stop drinking coffee cold turkey. That one lesson has stuck with me for twelve years. Not only did it lead to a switch from the roasted bean to dried leaf (the legal variety), but it also raised my money-spending awareness to a new level.

But this book is about time management, so let's talk about doing a Time Audit instead of a cash flow audit.

Unless you are different from most people, you won't initiate any significant changes in your life until you experience a crisis, or have a burning desire to change. Until you realize that your patterns are holding you back from achieving the success you want, all the advice in this book, along with the strategies, ideas, and tips, will be wasted. You will continue to repeat ineffective patterns, get the same results, and define your potential based on those results.

The Time Audit is designed to bring you face-to-face with your current patterns. Here's how it works:

1) For one week, you need to record every activity, phone call, interruption, and meeting you make or attend (see a sample audit on the following pages).

2) Then you will label each activity either as 'B' for Boulder (where you are working on completing a major project), as 'P' for Pebble (where you are working on a high-value task), or as 'S' for Sand.

This will be your personal current-reality picture. My guess is that, even if you complete the Time Audit for only one day, your patterns will be obvious (but one week is better). To get your electronic copy of the Time Audit chart, go online to the free resources in our Products section and download a simple Excel chart.[5] This is a neat tool that automatically calculates what percentage of your day is going to Boulders, Pebbles, and Sand. Simply keep it handy throughout the day and record what amount of time is being spent on your different activities.

> *Lots of folks confuse bad management with destiny.*
> –KIM HUBBARD, photography editor, Audubon

Whenever I introduce the Time Audit, two thoughts come to mind: 1) the powerful wake-up call I got when I first completed mine, and 2) that often we procrastinate about what we need the most. I hope you complete this simple exercise—even for one day—and get the same benefits I did!

If you do the Time Audit, you will see how your minutes can drift away without moving your Boulders ahead. It's a simple, easy wake-up call that I hope you will get.

---

5.   Go to www.hughculver.com/breakbook.

You can observe a lot by just watching.

—YOGI BERRA, former American Major
League Baseball player and manager

Sample Time Audit for three days

	MONDAY —Activity	B P S		TUESDAY —Activity	B P S		WEDNESDAY —Activity	B P S
7:30	email	P	7:30	email	S	7:30	plan	P
7:45	email	S	7:45	email	S	7:45	email	S
8:00	plan	P	8:00	plan	P	8:00		S
8:15	meeting	B	8:15	TM visit	P	8:15		S
8:30		B	8:30	TM visit	P	8:30	JR visit	S
8:45		B	8:45	sales call	P	8:45	email	P
9:00		B	9:00	sales call	P	9:00	paper wk	P
9:15	PV call	S	9:15	paper wk	P	9:15	paper wk	P
9:30	sales call	P	9:30		P	9:30	email	S
9:45	sales call	P	9:45		P	9:45	sales call	P
10:00	paper wk	S	10:00	meeting	B	10:00	sales call	P
10:15	updates	P	10:15		B	10:15	email	S
10:30	TM visit	S	10:30		B	10:30	TM visit	P
10:45	email	S	10:45		B	10:45	TM visit	P
11:00	paper wk	S	11:00	email	S	11:00	client call	P
11:15	paper wk	S	11:15		S	11:15	client call	P
11:30	JR visit	P	11:30	client call	P	11:30	paper wk	S
11:45	JR visit	P	11:45	client call	P	11:45	email	P
12:00	email	P	12:00	email	P	12:00	email	P
12:15		S	12:15		P	12:15	lunch	
12:30	lunch		12:30	lunch		12:30	lunch	
12:45	lunch		12:45	lunch		12:45	lunch	
13:00	plan	B	13:00	plan	P	13:00	meeting	P
13:15			13:15	JR visit	P	13:15		
13:30			13:30			13:30		
13:45			13:45			13:45		
14:00	meeting	P	14:00	meeting	P	14:00	email	P
14:15			14:15			14:15		
14:30			14:30			14:30	rtn calls	P
14:45			14:45	email	P	14:45		
15:00			15:00			15:00		
15:15			15:15			15:15	email	P
15:30			15:30			15:30		
15:45			15:45			15:45		
16:00			16:00			16:00		

Boulders and Pebbles Worksheet

What changes would you have to make, to enable you to work more on your Boulders, complete your Pebbles, and stay out of the Sandbox? Some examples:

1) I will use five minutes at the end of every day to plan my next day, with a focus on Boulders first.

2) In the morning, I will allow myself only twenty minutes on email, before concentrating on my Boulders, then return to email later.

3) I will stop my habit of jumping from task to task, and instead work on one thing until I come to a logical completion point.

4) I will close my door and let other people know that I prefer to deal with interruptions only after 10:30 am.

One change I will make as I plan my day is:

....

One change I will make at the start of my day is:

....

One activity I will have to stop doing is:

....

One change I will make in how I respond to interruptions is:

....

Now that you have had a look into your 'current reality' with the Time Audit, it's time to look at planning your future reality.

Focus on Boulders. Complete Pebbles.
Stay out of the Sandbox.

Goals Work (for You)

What man actually needs is not a tensionless state
but rather the striving and struggling for a worthwhile goal,
a freely chosen task.

—VIKTOR E. FRANKL, holocaust survivor, author of *Man's Search for Meaning*

Goals are the most important part of effective planning and predicting the future. Without goals, planning is nothing more than a 'wish list' written in vague language designed for happy procrastinators. Ask any successful person (and I don't just mean business success) and they will tell you about goals they set for themselves, whether for sports, finances, family, health, business achievement, or just plain fun.

When we create well-defined goals, whether they are to save more money, lose weight, increase our sales, or organize our office, we create new expectations and tension. The tension is between where we are now (our current reality) and where we want to go (our vision). This is a good thing! We need this tension to motivate us and to inspire us to overcome barriers and setbacks.

In the 1960s, Harvard researcher Hans Segle coined the term 'eustress' to refer to the good stress (tension) we experience when we are motivated and positively attracted to a result we want. Segle was looking at various external factors that created stress, or eustress.

Through his research, Segle was able to redefine how we think about stress; stress can be good, especially when we have a meaningful goal.

In a classic, twenty-year longitudinal study of Harvard Business School MBA graduates, researchers measured the general achievement level of graduates as they progressed in their careers, and compared these results to their stated goals upon graduation. The researchers divided the graduates into three groups:

- Those who had no goals upon graduation. These people might have stated their goal in a vague manner such as: "to get a good job that pays well."

- Those who had vague goals. They might have stated their goal as: "I am hoping to get into management with a medium-sized firm in the area of manufacturing, and I want to have a high income."

- Those who had specific goals, such as: "I want to get a job in fashion design that pays $50,000 to start, and where within five years I can move up to $100,000 with five weeks' vacation per year. I want to marry and have two children, and live in Westhaven." Understandably, this group comprised a mere three percent of the study group.

The results were nothing short of amazing. After twenty years, the second group (with vague goals) were, on average, 20% more successful than those who graduated with no goals at all. Not bad, but those turned out to be only modest successes, compared to the third group with specific goals.

The third group was *twice as successful* as the no-goals group in terms of wealth generation (earnings, investments, and assets), life-style (time off, holidays, and life experiences), happiness, and family. And it all started by turning on the brain's natural, new-expectation software, and letting the magic of eustress begin to do its work.

Maybe you are thinking you already know that goals work. Great, but are you using goals to their full benefit? In my businesses, I have seen goals turn crazy ideas into amazing results that created news internationally. At the same time, I have seen many frustrated entrepreneurs and employees drift through years of work without goals, direction, or motivation.

In all cases, goals—properly set and created with intention—are the one key factor that will always get you on a path to creating new success. "The best way to predict the future," as computer scientist and professor Alan Kay famously put it, "is to create it."

Here are three arguments for why goals work, and why I want you to re-visit your own goals:

Goals Help You Say 'No'

Does this sound familiar?

"Have you got just a minute?"

"Can I just ask you a quick question?"

"I just need a small favor . . . ."

If you are like most people, you hear lines like this all day long. Of course it is important to help others, but when you work from clear, motivating goals, you become more focused on completing your tasks and less willing to be pulled away from them. You can also be more assertive about saying 'No' to other people (and without remorse).

Darrell, an IT manager in a government department, oversees eight technicians who troubleshoot technology issues. When I met with the director of Darrell's department, he told me that, when Darrell is in the office, there is a constant lineup of staff, all wanting his help to resolve issues. Apparently, Darrell's open-door policy and helpful nature keeps him busy all day, answering questions from staff who should really be getting those answers on their own. But his generous time-sharing has a cost. Darrell was often the one coming in early and staying late. While the staff was obviously getting the quick advice and direction they wanted, Darrell was paying the cost, spending long hours catching up on his own work, and taking work home most evenings.

"Here's the surprising thing," continued the director. "When Darrell is out of the office, there is no lineup, and everyone seems to be able to get their work done!"

What's missing from this picture? Until Darrell revisits his goals and the most important objectives he is committed to, everyone else's objectives will become his.

> *We must not promise what we ought not, lest we be called on to perform what we cannot.*
> —ABRAHAM LINCOLN, 16th president of the United States

This is not to say that Darrell shouldn't own some responsibility for other people's needs in his department. But he also needs to have a goal of building their capacity to create solutions *on their own*.

There is a rule for this: "Those who don't have goals are ruled by those who do." In other words, if you don't start your day with a clear plan, then everyone else's emergencies often become yours. Sound familiar?

Think of all the interruptions you get in a day—how many of them are aligned with *your* goals and how many are only serving others? Having clear, compelling goals is the first step to creating the kind of day and success you want. Simple advice? Maybe, but worth repeating: Goals Work.

Goals Save You Time

When you did your Time Audit, you likely noticed (I know I did) that Sand finds a way to fill most of the cracks in your schedule. If you have ten minutes before a meeting starts, sand shows up with a bucketful of emails and phone messages. Hitting that energy slump around 11 am? Perfect—there's a sand-pile of paper on your desk to keep you busy, while Boulders, that need your attention, continue to be ignored.

Give me a stock clerk with a goal and I'll give you a man who will make history. Give me a man with no goals and I'll give you a stock clerk.

—J.C. PENNY, businessman and entrepreneur

When we have goals that motivate us, we naturally are more aware of our time and how we use it. When we first arrive at work, we are more committed to being efficient. We look for ways to keep meetings short. We become polite but efficient in conversations, and we find ways to save time when completing our email correspondence and doing other busy work.

Effective goals are time-bound. The challenge is to be effective with our time and, ideally, to find *new time* for high-value work or breaks.

Goals Help You Achieve More

'Someday' is a disease that will take your dreams to your grave with you.

—TIM FERRISS

When you set a goal for yourself, you always achieve more, even if you don't fully reach your goal. It's simply a matter of motivating your conscious thinking enough to beat out all the distractions.

Every time I commit to a triathlon competition or marathon run, for example, my workout patterns improve. I'm fitting in a run early before work, I'm watching what I eat, and paying more attention to sleep and stretching. This whole chain of new patterns was triggered by one event: making a goal and committing to it.

And here's a bonus: even if you don't quite reach your finish-time goal, you have still achieved more because of it. You probably have friends or family members who have committed to start training for their first 10K race, triathlon, or half-marathon, after going many years with only occasional exercise. Whatever happens (other than injury, of course), they always enjoy better health, more energy, and a positive experience, even though they rarely reach their performance goal on the day of the race. As soon as they commit to the goal, a whole chain of opportunities start to unfold to support their objective. Or, as Emerson more eloquently predicted: "Once you make a decision, the universe conspires to make it happen."

You and the Moon Mission

One of the more famous notions of Jim Collins, best-selling author of *Good to Great* and *Built to Last,* is that successful organizations have what he calls BHAGs, or Big Hairy Audacious Goals. "There is a difference between merely having a goal and becoming committed to a huge, daunting challenge, like a big mountain to climb," says Collins. Lesser objectives simply don't inspire or motivate the same way.

"President Kennedy and his advisors could have gone off into a conference room and drafted something like, 'Let's beef up the space program', or some other such vacuous statement," explains Collins. "Instead, Kennedy issued his BHAG ' . . . that this Nation should commit itself to achieving the goal, before this decade is out, of landing a man on the moon and returning him safely to earth'. The rest is history."

Have a look at your goals. Are they enough of a stretch? Do you get excited when you imagine working on them? Are they meaningful enough for you? If not, get to work on some new goals. As Abraham Lincoln (a man who knew much about

overcoming adversity with goals) once said, "A goal properly
set is halfway reached."

Goals vs. Flexibility

Perhaps you are thinking, "I don't want to be one of those people
who are constantly looking at their watches and fretting about
goals." I agree—the objective of having goals is not to become so
results-focused that you cannot engage in the occasional distraction or 'down time'.

Goals are about accomplishing what is most important, so that
you are able to get the benefits of those results and have reflection
time, planning time, or simply do-nothing time. In fact, my experience has been that, when I work from goals, I create even more
opportunities for spontaneity, fun, and time away from work.

At some point, we've all had that feeling of dread—we have too
much to do. It could sweep across you as you review your day planner, or as you look at your bulging Inbox, with unread emails that
might as well be archived, they are so old. Or you could feel it as you
return home after a frenetic day of dealing with what Stephen Covey
would call Quadrant III activities: urgent, but not important.

The brain loves to ruminate on what's wrong. And the dread of
unfinished work gives your brain a lot to attend to; and it will. You
will worry, have anxiety, and stay busy.

Goals, well designed, get you focused on what needs to be done.
You have a plan and, if you follow it, you will reap the benefits of
knowing when to work and when not to. You can be assured that
there is a game plan to rely on, and that it's okay to turn work off,
be with the family, and recharge.

Dopamine and Goals

We now know that the neurotransmitter, Dopamine, is the secret juice we create when we anticipate some good event. Often referred to as the neurotransmitter of anticipation, Dopamine is responsible for that Christmas Eve buzz that keeps children awake far too late, and the nervous excitement of young lovers preparing for a first date. Once we focus on a goal that we want, the body goes to work and uses Dopamine to heighten our anticipation and attention.

If you have a plan you are eighty percent certain of, you should violently execute it.
—GEORGE PATTON, U.S. general in World War II

I often use this internal switch to my advantage in seminars, by announcing the 'exciting' lesson or training video that will follow the break. It often surprises me, but just hearing the announcement gets more people back in the room on time. You can use it as well.

When you have a goal that you are excited about, the body's wiring is ready to help you get there. But you need to give it a picture to focus on. It's no different than imagining the beaches of Cabo San Lucas before you actually arrive. The image of endless stretches of sun-soaked sand on the Baja Peninsula excites and energizes you to put in the extra effort to get your work wrapped up. By staying focused on your dream, you are able to head off on your vacation without worries and guilt-free.

Take a moment to create either a physical image (download a picture off the Internet or use pictures from magazines) or a mental image of one of your goals. I usually imagine crossing Pebbles off in my day planner, and feeling complete when I pack up at the end of a day. Let this image develop in your mind, so you can recall it at any time. And use it to pull you out of energy slumps or to recharge you when it feels like progress is elusive.

It's like the turbocharger on my car's little diesel engine. It's always there, waiting to be used, to give me a boost in power. But I have to intentionally engage it to get the extra power I need on the hill.

Get clear on your vision, return to it often, and let your internal programming help get you to the beach.

Setting Smart Goals

People are not planning for retirement. Every year, the Royal Bank of Canada surveys Canadians to measure their readiness for retirement. And the results are dismal. A meagerly 38% have a solid, substantial financial plan for creating the savings they want for their golden years. Another third of Canadians have no plan at all. Not only do they not have a plan, they are probably too late to create the savings needed. But it gets worse.

The remaining one-third of Canadians have a plan, but not one that a financial expert would deem sufficient to ensure a similar quality of living after retirement. And a full 13% of them have included winning the lottery as a part of their strategy!

We have all had times where we missed the target and didn't create the results that we wanted. It could be the Valentine's Day card we meant to buy and only remembered when our spouse or partner handed us the card they *did* remember to get. Or some work-related target like increased sales, coaching for staff, or improved marketing that somehow slipped by and didn't materialize.

It might be that the problem is the goal itself. A poor goal will always lead to poor results.

The classic acronym SMART is a good starting place for improving your goal-setting habits. For years, this simple formula has been invaluable as a quick checklist for me on my own goal-setting activities. It's also the formula to use when delegating to staff, or designing team goals, or coaching employees (or even with your children!).

S is for Specific

Before you start, you need to know what you are creating. All too often, I hear the most incredibly vague goals from people, like, "I need to improve the way I communicate," or "I have to deal with interruptions better." On the surface there is nothing wrong with these goals—that is, until you try to keep them!

You have probably been in planning meetings where there was a lot of excited conversation about the need to improve some process, such as communications or customer service. At the end of the conversation, there seemed to be an agreement: something needed to be done

> *Nothing is particularly hard if you divide it into smaller jobs.*
> —HENRY FORD, founder of the Ford Motor Company

to improve the situation, and so a line was added to the To-Do list that said, "Improve communications." Inevitably, one month later nothing had changed. The goal is simply too vague.

Being specific requires work. After you identify the need for change, improvement, or growth, you need to narrow the focus to a specific outcome. For example, "improving communication" could actually be stated as, "finishing every planning meeting with a specific list of tasks, each with accountabilities and deadlines." Or it could be something like this: "Every Friday, Jim will circulate an email with the sales numbers recorded for that week." Saying "I will improve communications" is akin to saying "I will get richer"; it's hard to measure, and even harder to know what to work on.

One of the greatest benefits of a goal is the process of writing it. If you follow the model I present here, then there is a certain degree of rigor required and gaps in logic or direction will quickly become apparent. Defining a specific desired outcome also requires you to organize and evaluate options and to prioritize the outcomes you want. Not only does this lead to better outcomes, but it forces you to decide what is ultimately important. Try this now: take an objective or goal that you have, but have not yet completed. Write down a description of the goal and then compare it to the model on these pages. Is it specific? Does it motivate you? Is it realistic?

Use these questions to evaluate other goals, and to learn how to craft goals that are realistic and objective. The better your goals, the better your outcomes; it's that simple.

M is for Measurable

There has to be a measurable outcome for every goal. Without some kind of metric of success, your goals are just hopeful wishes. The measure can be the number of sales calls you will make this week, the amount of time you dedicate to the marketing strategy, the amount of time you commit to cleaning your office, or the number of work-free evenings you will enjoy this week.

Just like an athlete, setting a specific performance target is critical for being accountable, and for creating more success. Without a number attached to the goal, we can easily convince ourselves that we have achieved enough. But when you add a measure to your goal, you immediately raise the stakes and start to work toward better results.

A good rule of thumb is that there has to be a number in your SMART goal. Here are some weak goals that are not measurable, followed by improved versions:

Weak: **Get better at managing my time.**
Better: Every Friday at 4 pm, spend fifteen minutes planning the next week.

Weak: **Learn how to use my email software better.**
Better: On Thursday, get Jerry to show me how to set up rules and folders and empty my Inbox.

Weak: **Take better care of myself.**
Better: Four times a week after work, walk for twenty-five minutes.

A is for Achievable

A good goal should set us up for success. For example, if you want to get into better physical shape, first create a goal that you know you can reach within one week, such as "no snacking after 8:00 pm this week." After you achieve that goal, create a harder goal. By continuing, in this increasingly harder goal-setting pattern, you are teaching yourself a powerful lesson: you keep goals.

R is for Risky

Good goals will stretch and challenge you. Notice the difference between the following two goals:

1) "I commit to spending two hours a month coaching my staff."

2) "I will create a coaching contract with each person on staff. This will include at least one thirty-minute coaching conversation with each person each month. This is a six-month trial commitment."

The first example is a goal, but the target is pretty low. The second goal would stretch any leader and be easy to measure: you either did it or you didn't.

When you create a risky goal, you activate a part of the brain that is competitive and risk-averse. This part of the brain is hyper-aware of things relating to risk, and it seeks ways to minimize them. So, when you find yourself negotiating the dark alleys in a foreign city trying to find your hotel, it will marshal hormones, endorphins, and adrenalin to prepare you for perceived danger. In a similar way, when you create a risky goal for yourself, this part of the brain will want to find solutions that mitigate the risk.

> *Luck is a matter of preparation meeting opportunity.*
>
> —OPRAH, television host, producer, and philanthropist

When I committed to compete in my fourth Ironman competition, it was a risk. Not a risk with physical danger, but a risk in terms of fitting in sufficient training for an ultra-distance event when I already had a full personal and work schedule. Unlike my previous Ironman events, I now had young children at home and a wife who worked. I owned a busy company, worked long hours, traveled about ten times a month, and sat on two volunteer boards. Time was tight and I didn't have extra time for the rigorous training regimen needed for an Ironman. Yet I knew I needed to stay motivated with my exercise, so I made the commitment anyway.

Once I committed to the new goal, I started to notice a variety of unique and fortuitous opportunities to fit in training workouts.

After a presentation, I would sometimes quickly change and get in a short workout before my flight home. Often I would run to work or combine a bike ride with errands. I changed my sleep patterns to go to bed earlier, get up earlier and do my workout in the morning before anyone else in the house woke up.

I was truly amazed to find that, despite my workload and other commitments, I was able to average more than thirty-five hours of training per month in the four months leading up to the Ironman. While this will seem paltry compared to some serious competitors, it was almost double the workout volume I had averaged in the previous six months. And I have been able to maintain that target, or more, every month since.

T is for Time-Bound

The final part of the SMART formula is to add a time factor to every goal. You should be asking: "What date will motivate me, allow me to get the work done on time, and make it less likely that I will procrastinate?" Human nature is such that we are more likely to overestimate our abilities and not allow enough time. On the other hand, allowing too much time might mean there is less motivation to get the project moving towards completion.

When I am working with teams, I encourage them to set the most realistic time goals they can, based on their knowledge of competing demands, workload, etc. And I ask them to commit to renegotiating dates, if necessary, not simply pushing dates back when they run out of time. Renegotiating means that you, or the team, have to do more than simply postpone the date. Postponing deadlines can lead to a disastrous pattern of putting off the inevitable. A better strategy is to change the date *and* to make some other change to ensure that the goal is achieved. You might need to assign more help to the goal, move some other goal, break the goal into small parts, delegate internally, or outsource some of the work.

The good news is that, the more times you set and achieve your goals, the more likely you will be to continue creating—and achieving—goals in the future.

A quick review

Before we get to the worksheet, here is a quick reminder of the SMART goals formula:

Specific – Have you got a clear definition of outcomes?

Measurable – Can this goal be measured?

Achievable – Will it be obvious when you are successful?

Risky – Is this a stretch goal that will build your success?

Time-Bound – Do you have a deadline for achieving your goal?

When I teach our seminar, I always have participants share their commitments with a partner. That partner's role is to listen carefully, and then ask good coaching-type questions (open-ended) to help refine the new commitments. Some of the typical questions asked are:

"By when will you have started that goal?"
"How will you know that you have reached the goal?"
"Who do you need to help you with this goal?"
"What is the first step you need to make in order to get started?"
"What is the most likely barrier you will encounter and how will you overcome it?"

Ask yourself these questions now. This is a great way to catch any vague language and to think through the execution of the goal. Ultimately, every goal that goes through this filter improves.

You can reproduce this conversation at your office or, if you are self-employed, with a colleague. Make it a reciprocal agreement— you ask for help with your new goals and offer to help them with theirs. Ideally, schedule a check-in date to reconnect and review progress.

Smart Goals Worksheet

This is a good chance for you to practice writing SMART goals. You might be surprised to discover that it's not easy, but give it a try. First, write an objective that you would like to set. Don't worry about the format—just capture the idea here:

....

....

Next, rewrite this objective as a SMART goal, paying particular attention to making it specific and having a measurable outcome.

Goal #1: ....

....

Finally, who can support you in reaching this goal? I find that sharing my goals with someone I know, who will hold me accountable, greatly increases my success.

....

Following this same process, write two more goals as SMART goals.

Goal #2: ....

....

Support person is: ....

Goal #3: ....

....

Support person is: ....

Part II

• • •

SYSTEMS

Rewiring your programs
to create more success

*The person who never made a mistake
never tried anything new.*

—ALBERT EINSTEIN, theoretical physicist

Systems for Success

Be sceptical of your stories:
I don't necessarily agree with everything I say.

—MARSHALL MCLUHAN, Canadian educator,
philosopher, and scholar

Okay, time for a tour. Please take a minute to look around the room you are in. Whether you are hanging out in a café, in your home, or sitting on a bus, just have a quick scan.

Notice the orientation of your chair to the door, the windows, the table, etc. If in your office, take note of the location of your paperwork, phone, pens, and anything you rely on to do your work. If you are in a café, take note of how it is organized to manage traffic flow and allow for product sales.

Inherently, all of the pieces of a room make up a system. And that system influences what can happen in that room, what can't, and what is downright awkward. For example, you can maneuver easily between furniture, but it's pretty hard to cross the room *through* a desk. The furniture, in effect, guides where you go; it becomes a part of the system you work within.

Other examples of systems are roadways and street signs, your banking accounts, the lights in your house, meetings, and day planners. Just as you are influenced by the design of each system, if the system were to change, your patterns would naturally change with it.

Examples of company-instituted systems are all around us: performance management and incentive plans, documentation and filing, ordering and accounting, and even systems to promote creative thinking (companies like 3M and Google famously encourage innovation by allowing some employees time to work on projects of their choosing).

Forms and templates you use in your work are examples of systems—their design influences what you do. If you were to improve a form (such as your invoice template or order form), naturally you would have to change the way you enter the data. Over time, the results could be dramatic in amount of time saved, reduced aggravation, and reallocation of your resources. It is only a form, but that one small change could reap long-term benefits.

I get excited about systems (strange, but true) because I only have to change them once, and then they start to work for me. Consider how drive-through restaurants, bank ATMs, and self-service checkout lines at grocery stores have meant less wait time for consumers and have improved the bottom line for many companies. Online shopping for books, travel, cameras, shoes, and even finding a date are all examples of new systems that have transformed how we can do routine activities.

In this chapter, we look at five important systems. These could lead to company-wide system changes, or the change could simply start with you. They are:

1) **Plan like a Pilot** – *Why and how you need to plan for the week*

2) **You Come First** – *Reducing interruptions so you can focus on Boulders*

3) **Putting Meetings on a Diet** – *Maximizing the benefits of meetings*

4) **Exorcise Your Email** – *Using email as a tool, not a time-filler*

5) **Clearing the Clutter** – *Reducing distractions and increasing focus*

First up is a re-think about what you focus on during the week.

1

● ● ●

Plan like a Pilot

*Life is what happens to you
while you're busy making other plans.*

–JOHN LENNON, songwriter

Confession time: I have been hired to lead at least one hundred strategic planning sessions for corporate, government, and not-for-profit organizations. I have worked with some of the most ambitious, brightest, and talented leaders in industries ranging from high tech to health care, and they are all the same. What I mean is that they all fall into the same trap—and I am guilty of leading them there.

They love to create big, ambitious goals (remember Jim Collin's BHAG?). They usually do a brilliant job of defining the goal, the people who are accountable, and even the milestones. And then they stop. The goals go into a nice report that gets circulated, and everyone nods in collective agreement. After that, in an ongoing flurry of putting out fires and new initiatives, the goals are rarely mentioned, except at quarterly reviews, but by then, the focus is likely to be on new goals.

Okay, to be fair, lots of movement usually occurs, and many goals do get completed. But for the most part, there is a disconnect between the momentum experienced in the planning stage and the daily activity that makes up the organization's success. Great intentions are swallowed up in the day-to-day malaise of distractions. While you are fussing over urgent client requests or staffing issues, you are usually not looking at the strategic plan created at the retreat six months ago.

The problem is not so much lack of *intention*; it is more an issue of *perspective*. The planning retreat was all about the coming years, or year. The crisis on Tuesday is all about Tuesday. So when you are putting out the fire about late shipments, it's hard to be thinking about the new scheduling software that you were talking about last September.

In his book, *First Things First,* Stephen Covey likens the problem to trying to walk down the street while looking through the telephoto lens of a camera. You have an intense focus on what is right in front of you, but miss out on a larger perspective.

To solve this problem, you need a more workable, action-oriented, perspective, which is (drum roll please): the week. Okay, I know this doesn't sound revolutionary, but stick with me. This is actually the most revolutionary change my clients make—in planning, and in how they think about time.

When you plan for the week, you can include long-term strategies and goals along with the more immediate needs of the day. We call this the Action Plan, because it is all about what is going to create the action for you to move your Boulders forward.

In my work, moving Boulders forward, toward completion, can translate into more sales, better staff performance, lower costs, fewer missed deadlines, and (best of all) less stress for me. Boulders can also include coaching staff, resolving conflicts, improving customer service, and other non-sales-related and non-client-related goals.

Creating a list of high-priority goals for the week will be one of your most valuable systems. It will keep you on track with what is important, and help to prevent you from spending time on low-priority Sandbox tasks. Your Action Plan will give you targets to work toward, and a reason to get back on course after every interruption. It will also break the larger Boulders down into Pebbles, making previously daunting tasks more achievable.

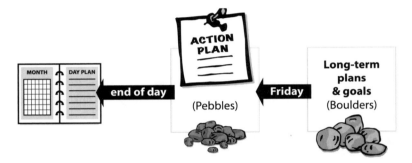

The definitions:

Your **Action Plan** – records the major achievements you will complete this week.

Your **Day Plan** – records the Pebbles planned for today.

There are four steps to creating your Action Plan:

1) **Review last week's Action Plan.** I recommend that you allow at least fifteen minutes for this exercise every Friday afternoon. This is a good time to stop, review, decide what items you want to transfer forward to the next week, and what items you want to drop. There are at least four choices you can make with each decision:

- **Do it now.** Here's a quick rule of thumb: If you estimate that the task can be completed in less than two minutes, don't bother recording it on your Day Plan. Simply complete the task and move on.

- **Defer it.** Later today? Record it on your Day Plan. Later this week? Record it on your Action Plan.

- **Delegate it.** Use this as an opportunity to train or coach someone else on your team or to outsource the work.

- **Dump it.** Decide that this is not important and cross it out.

2) **Identify** the Boulders that you want to complete, or to move ahead to next week. This is your chance to reflect on your progress with long-term goals, and to look at what you need to get done. If you did not manage to complete a certain Pebble last week, it may not have been presented in achievable, bite-sized chunks. Next, add personal goals for the week. This is the time to commit to your dinner date with your partner/spouse, exercise, or register for that evening course.

   Warning: Avoid the mistake of making the Action Plan another shopping list of miscellaneous tasks screaming for attention. Your Action Plan for the week should only list major, high-priority tasks. I recommend that your list has no more than twelve items—anything more and you risk losing focus.

3) **Define** the list, to make sure it is full of SMART goals. All five elements of the SMART acronym are excellent. (Forgot what they are? Go to page 74 to refresh your memory.)

I Can See Clearly Now . . .

When defining your goals for the week, make sure they are Clear, Appealing, and Realistic. Pay close attention to these three elements:

Clear – Does each item on the list provide clear direction, enabling you to begin immediately? Remember that a goal properly set is halfway reached. Set yourself up for success by taking an extra minute of planning time to record each item carefully. Three days from now, a vague ambition will become a procrastinator's dream, and it will likely be skipped over in favor of more urgent needs.

Appealing – Have you written each Pebble in such a way that you will enjoy working on it, and completing it? Get into the practice of writing Action Plan goals as small chunks of work, clearly defined, and inviting to work on. Instead of writing, "Work on competitor research," try restating the goal as something you will be more likely to work on: "Call Jim and get his support on competitor research."

Realistic – Can you accomplish every Pebble in your Action Plan this week, while still allowing for interruptions? You will be better off completing a modest Action Plan and enjoying that success, than to write endlessly long lists that only get partially completed. Focus only on the work that must be done this week.

Here are three examples of Boulder-style goals written in an intimidating, unclear manner, and then changed into Clear, Appealing, and Realistic Pebbles:

Poorly written objective: Resolve personality issues with the committee.
Better objective: Call Tom on Tuesday and get advice, suggest some one-on-one coaching.

Poorly written objective: Meet with Anne-Marie to resolve issue with poor sales tracking.
Better objective: Meet with Anne-Marie and coach her on proper use of Excel.

Poorly written objective: Review marketing plan.
Better objective: Call Jim and get copy of last year's marketing plan. Brainstorm draft outline of new plan for thirty minutes.

4) Post – Make sure your list is visible, where you can refer to it throughout the day. You can post the list at your desk, in your Day-Timer, or in Microsoft Outlook Tasks.

Welcome to Categories

Outlook Tasks is a great place to record and keep track of your Action Plan, especially if you learn how to use Categories (note that to view categories you have to make a one-time selection by clicking on *View > Arrange by > Categories*).[6]

You start by creating your own list of Categories (to do this, right-click on any Task and *select Categorize > All Categories > New > enter new name > OK*). And every time you create a new Task, select the category you want it listed in.[7]

At a minimum, I would create a Category called "@Boulders" for all upcoming Boulders, and one called "@Action Plan" for the Pebbles you are working on this week (note that including @ in front of a name will keep it at the top of your list).

When you arrive at work Monday morning and review the Action Plan you prepared on Friday afternoon, you will be focused and excited about starting to work on your goals. Participants in our *Reclaiming the Clock* seminars tell us that adopting the Action

---

6.   Categories are shown in a selection box in the bottom right corner of the new Task form in Outlook 2003, and in the top right corner in Outlook 2007.
7.   The shortcut keys for creating a new Task are CTRL+SHIFT+K.

Plan system is one of the most important (and simplest) improvements to their time-effectiveness—at work and at home.

Mondays are for recruiting . . .

Here is a neat idea used by John, a division director at Investors Group (a national financial advice firm in Canada), that is worth considering for anyone trying to balance competing objectives in their week.

When John plans his week, he designates each day with a different theme. Mondays are for recruiting new consultants— having a successful consultant team is critical for his sales growth.

Tuesdays and Thursdays are for appointments with his clients. Wednesdays are open-door days for trouble shooting, coaching, and supporting his team. Fridays are reserved for professional development and internal meetings.

As John explained, what started as a survival solution to the unpredictable needs of his consultants has become a winning strategy for focusing, and for forcing others to work around his priorities.

Creating Your Day Plan

Our twelve seat de Havilland Twin Otter had just taken off from Inuvik, in the northern Yukon Territories, heading to the Firth River for ten days of magical wilderness river rafting. Flying in a bush plane in the Arctic, across endless miles of open tundra, is a remarkable adventure in itself. Especially when you are loaded to the roof with rolled-up rafts, life jackets, camping gear, food and duffle bags, in addition to twelve anxious and slightly nauseous guests.

By map, our destination was a straight line, heading roughly southwest, across vast reaches of open tundra, to the headwaters of the river. But bush planes never fly in a straight line. In fact, one of our pilots admitted that they are usually off-course more than 50% of the time. Does this sound like a typical day in your office?

The pilot (or the autopilot on bigger planes) is constantly adjusting direction and altitude, based on weather conditions, geography of the land (small, low-flying planes don't like mountains), and proximity to other aircraft. In a small plane

> *Plan your work, work your plan.*
> –ANONYMOUS

like the Twin Otter, this constant maneuvering and bouncing is obvious, less so in a big commercial jet. So how is it that the plane always arrives at its destination?

Simply put: pilots always work from a flight plan (think Action Plan) and, when pushed off course, they always return to the flight plan. It would be ridiculous for a pilot to take off from the airport, thinking, "I'll just see how it goes today," or to base a trip on how everyone is feeling that day. Instead, pilots have a flight plan that keeps their focus on the ultimate goal.

Why should your approach to work be any different?

I have just introduced the Action Plan, the best way I know of creating a meaningful, focused flight plan from long-term objectives. Now it is time to create your plan for the day. We call this your Day Plan.

And Now, the Day Plan

The Day Plan will become your most important tool for staying focused, but it must be created with care. The worst mistake I see is making an overly-ambitious To-Do list of un-prioritized, miscellaneous tasks that compete for your attention.

Take the time to avoid the "garbage in, garbage out" syndrome, and you will have an efficient system that will serve you well, even in the most harried, crazy-busy times. As Ben Franklin said more than 300 years ago, "An ounce of prevention is worth a pound of cure."

Here are the four steps to creating your Day Plan:

1) **Review:** set aside about ten minutes at the end of your day to review your Action Plan. What got started? What got completed? What got ignored?

2) **Identify:** choose the pebbles that must get completed the following day. Be decisive; don't make this an exercise in copying from day to day. Instead, choose to either: Do it, Defer it, Delete it, or Dump it.

Stop!

By now you might have made a classic mistake: you mysteriously just designed a twelve-hour workday (not including interruptions). Everything looks important, and because it was on your list yesterday, it is magically reappearing on your Day Plan for tomorrow. Sound familiar? There is a solution.

Instead of creating a gargantuan list that will realistically never get done in a day, make some decisions. Can you complete any tasks immediately? Often I find that I just need to send off a quick email request to delegate a task, or that I can simply delete a low-value item. In just two minutes, I can deal with an annoying reminder that has been migrating from Tuesday to Wednesday to Thursday. Do yourself a favor: look for quick solutions, and keep your Day Plan short.

3) **Define:** prioritize this list with an "A" for Pebbles that must get done first. That's it. Don't waste your time prioritizing the whole list, or calculating what portion of an hour each task will take to complete. Just mark "A" for what needs to get done first.

Most days, I will have between three and five "A" items on my list. Any more than that and I need to examine how I am prioritizing, or get help.

Start each day by reviewing your Action Plan and your Day Plan. Then, throughout the day, especially in the morning and right after lunch, update your plans.

Keep both your Action Plan and your Day Plan visible all day, and work from them. Now here is a great secret that serves me, and my clients, well. After you come back from a meeting, or finish a conference call, or send off the updated report for review, return first to your Action Plan, not to your Day Plan. Maintaining your focus on the objectives for the week reminds you of what is most important, and ensures you stay focused on Boulders.

As you find yourself mired in the chaos and distractions of your day, this simple refocus will pay big dividends. Just like a pilot, your flight plan (Action Plan) is ultimately all that matters.

4) **Post:** keep your list visible and take pleasure in crossing Pebbles off your list.

Action Plan Worksheet

Changing the way you organize your work requires a new system, a commitment to follow that system, and the habit of using it daily. Now is the time to make some commitments to your new system.

On the worksheet below, fill in some commitments that you are prepared to make to ensure that your new system will be successful. Here are some examples:

✓ I will create new Categories in Outlook Tasks for Boulders, Action Plans, Personal, etc. (remember to change your View setting to '*View > Arrange by > Category*').

✓ I will block ten minutes on Fridays to create my Action Plan for the following week.

✓ I will block ten minutes every afternoon to create my Day Plan for the next day.

✓ I will keep my Action Plan and Day Plan visible.

✓ After an interruption, I will first review my Action Plan for the week.

....

....

....

....

....

....

....

....

2

You Come First

You can't always get what you want, but if you try sometimes, well you just might find, you get what you need.

—ROLLING STONES, "You can't always get what you want"

"Have you got a minute?"

Based on the feedback we get in our training programs, the three biggest thieves of time are email, meetings, and interruptions. Interruptions may be considered normal for your workday, but they break your concentration and slow your progress. In fact, most people greatly underestimate the impact of interruptions. When the phone call takes you away from the spreadsheet you are working on, your brain goes as well. Unlike a computer, it takes time and effort to return to what you were originally working on. And often, we never return.

In one study on time management, researchers observed that the average worker was interrupted every eight to twelve minutes. It took between four and ten minutes to complete the interruption—using the minimum numbers, that's over ten weeks of lost time a year! But here's the kicker: according to research by Charge Foundation, 40% of the time, the interrupted person never returned to the original task.[8] Like a pinball, where someone else is pushing the flipper button, we bounce from task to task without finishing anything we start.

In a separate study, researchers Gloria Mark and Victor Gonsalez of the University of California, Irvine, found that workers they studied were switching activities from working on a document to speaking with a colleague to making a call on average *every three minutes*. And, once interrupted, it took workers twenty-five minutes to return to the original task, if they returned at all.[9]

Remember that in the "Where Does the Time Go?" chapter, we estimated that a total of one hour of interruptions each day is the equivalent of six weeks of lost time each year—and for most people I work with, this estimate is low. Limiting interruptions means you get more Pebbles completed, move your Boulders forward, and enjoy more control over your day.

Experiment with the following approaches—they all work, but you need to find the ones that work best in your situation. I suggest that you try each new approach for one week and notice the difference. Some improvement? Great, keep going. No change? Okay, try a different approach.

Google's Pac-Man logo costs millions
To celebrate the thirtieth anniversary of the iconic Pac-Man computer game, Google posted their logo as an operational Pac-Man game for one Friday in May, 2010. One estimate is

8.   Betty Lin-Fisher, *Houston Chronicle*, 2/27/2006
9.   Researchers, Gloria Mark and Victor Gonzalez, of the University of California, Irvine, as reported in the *Houston Chronicle*, 2/27/2006

that the one-half billion visitors to the Google search engine that day stayed (and played?) an average of thirty-six seconds longer. Doing the math, and using twenty-five dollars per hour as the wage rate, Google's whimsical celebration led to some $120M lost time that day. That's the equivalent of 20,000 people working for six weeks—that's a lot of productivity!

Now imagine how much time is lost to the occasional view of a YouTube video, Facebook entry, funny email, or flash web page advertisement![10]

Time Boundaries

When I moved to Kelowna, in British Columbia, I wanted to start working with a financial planner to help me with my savings plan. After unsuccessfully trying to find a day for our first meeting, I suggested a Thursday afternoon. "Sorry," he said. "I don't have appointments on Thursday afternoons. That's my time to read and study the markets."

> *The mirror will always reveal to you the number one interrupter in your life.*
>
> –JOHN ADAIR, television host, author

When I expressed my surprise at his discipline, he replied, "Would you rather work with an advisor who spends all his time with clients, or with one who takes time every week to study the markets and to learn as much as possible to serve you better?"

Good point!

Creating Time Boundaries is about being proactive—before others gobble your minutes, like a game of Pac-Man, with their crises. Remember the rule: "Those who don't have goals are ruled by

---

10. http://blog.rescuetime.com/2010/05/24/the-tragic-cost-of-google-pac-man-4-82-million-hours/

those who do." I find that Time Boundaries are a critical technique for protecting my time and exercising control over my calendar.

Examples of good Time Boundaries include:

- Time blocked to work on a Boulder. Even blocking twenty minutes can be enough to move the Boulder forward, for example, by defining some specific Pebbles and then delegating them to others.

- Thirty minutes once a week for planning, contemplation, or professional-development reading.

- Time to return client phone calls (mornings are best) every Monday, Tuesday, and Wednesday.

- Time once a week for creative thinking and for reviewing systems in your office.

In his book, **First Things First**, *Stephen Covey suggests that we ask this powerful question: "What is one thing that I am* **not** *doing now, but if I did it well and consistently, it would make a significant difference to my work?" This question motivated me to dedicate more time for research and writing (and you are reading one of the results). How would you answer his question?*

- Time to resolve a communications issue with a colleague.

- Time to plan for your next team meeting, so that it can be more than just a review of what's going on.

- Time every afternoon to review and update your Day Plan.

- Time every Friday to clear off your desk, do filing, and prepare your Action Plan for the following week.

- Time for physical exercise: a brisk walk around the block, combining an errand with a break to get some fresh air, or stretching at your desk.

Be Honest

If you only have a few minutes, let the other person know this at the start of the conversation. If the interruption is important and needs more time, suggest that you schedule a time to meet later.

© Randy Glasbergen.
www.glasbergen.com

GLASBERGEN

"No matter how busy I am, I'm never too busy to stop and complain about how busy I am."

While this new practice might seem blunt at first, think of it instead as simply being honest. My guess is that, if the other person told you she didn't have time at this moment, you would respect it. So why not take the lead and be honest about your needs?

Learn to Say 'No'

One of the classic mistakes many people at work make is to be available all the time. This can lead to staff members becoming overly dependent and to you being frustrated. And it can lead to heightened stress levels, lower productivity, and unrealistic expectations.

When you say 'No' to people, you are not abandoning them—you are merely declaring your boundaries and avoiding unclear expectations.

Unplug

If you are working on a difficult problem or need space for creative thinking, take your work into a different room. This is one of my favorite solutions: I have found that if I go across the street to a local café with my laptop (and no cell phone), I can be twice as productive for creative writing, planning, or just thinking. The walk to the café, the change in setting, and the background sounds all seem to stimulate creative work.

It might be that leaving the office for sojourns to cafés is not possible, but how about just moving to a different workspace in your building?

If you are often interrupted during the day, allow for that time when you are planning your day. In other words, if you tend to only have about three uninterruped hours of work time in a day, then try to schedule only that much work. Your objective should be to cross off as many Pebbles as possible on your list, not to have a huge carry-over to the next day.

No More Bandaids

To create permanent solutions to some interruptions, look for opportunities to train people or to document answers to typical questions.

For example, in our office we have a Systems Binder. Any time that we notice recurring questions or the need for certain information to be shared among staff, it gets recorded in the Systems Binder. Here are some examples:

- Passwords to software and computers.

- Self-help instructions for common computer woes.

- Favorite hotels for traveling.

- Frequent flyer numbers, customer service phone numbers for airlines, and a record of flight credits.

- A list of meeting room venues, with meeting room sizes, prices, and phone numbers.

- Routines for booking e-learning clients and for setting up usernames and passwords.

- Instructions for using our shopping-cart software.

Not only are these notes useful for us, they are a perfect resource for new or temporary staff.

The Two-Minute Rule

What requests, from other people, break up your day? They can include requests from your boss, colleagues, customers, or emails that need your attention. The problem with stopping what you are doing and reacting to these interruptions is that you will forever be distracted from your Day Plan. Instead, try practicing the Two-Minute Rule:

- If an interruption will take two minutes or less, just do it. Don't bother recording it, scheduling it, or coming back to it. Simply stop what you are doing, complete the phone call or email or whatever, and get back to what you were working on.

- Otherwise, schedule it. Record the task in your Day Plan for later that day, in your Action Plan for later that week, or for some future date.

I estimate that, in a typical day, I have forty to fifty unplanned interruptions. Of those, about one-half can be completed in less than two minutes. Good examples are when a client requests a  document, or our printer calls with a question. These tasks I do immediately. There is usually no need to record them or schedule them. I simply take care of them and move on.

Anything that requires more time, I schedule to do later in the day (Day Plan) or later in the week (Action Plan). By following the Two-Minute Rule, I am being selective about what I allow to interrupt my flow, and I am sticking to my planning tools, so that nothing gets lost and my desk isn't littered with reminders on sticky notes and scraps of paper.

Interruptions Worksheet

Changing how you respond to interruptions can have an incredible impact on your productivity and sense of accomplishment in the day. What system changes do you need to make so that you can follow your plans more effectively? How are you going to measure results (for example, by recording the time saved in one day)?

One change I need to make when dealing with unwanted interruptions is:

....

....

....

....

For one week I am going to practice:

....

....

....

....

I am going to measure my results by:

....

....

....

....

....

3

$\bullet \quad \bullet \quad \bullet$

Putting Meetings on a Diet

*Meetings are indispensable
when you don't want to do anything.*

—JOHN KENNETH GALBRAITH,
economist and author

Meetings can provide an invaluable opportunity for information-sharing, decision-making, and generating new ideas, but they can also be a huge waste of time. In fact, in a survey by Office Team of more than 600 office workers in the United States, the majority of respondents said that meetings were their biggest time-waster.

Jason Fried, simplification advocate and co-founder of 37signals, has an interesting rationale for why he abhors team meetings. He thinks of a one-hour meeting with six people attending as really being a six-hour event (because that's the financial cost to the company). The sheer thought of that investment is enough to limit company meetings to an absolute minimum, and keep them off his agenda completely.

One of my seminar participants complained about her Olympian-like seven-meeting days. She said that, not only was it challenging to have that many meetings in a day, but the last fifteen minutes of each meeting were wasted while she mentally prepared for the next meeting. You may not have seven meetings in a day, but even one a week can provide an opportunity to make that time more effective.

When meetings are inefficient, they waste time and lead to poor results. Worse, they create negative expectations for future meetings. People start to dread going to them, and invitees mysteriously become unavailable or simply do not show up.

Based on my observations with hundreds of clients, the most common meeting failures are caused by:

- Agendas not created, poorly written, or not circulated in advance

- Objectives being unclear or not followed

- Meetings starting late or going overtime

- People distracted by laptop computers or cell phones

- Presenters not being prepared

- People not contributing, due to a lack of trust or role confusion

- Participants taking the conversation off-topic

- Disagreements or personal attacks that don't get addressed and resolved

- The same topics continually reappearing without decisions being reached

- Unclear commitments, and/or promises not kept

Here are my twelve best solutions for putting meetings on a diet.

As with all of my tips and techniques, your job is to find one or two solutions that you will commit to using for one month.

You may not chair the meetings you attend, but you can still influence their quality. Start by getting consensus on the overall objectives of your meeting. Even the most ineffective chairperson will readily agree that holding an effective meeting is a common goal.

1) **Don't go.** Your time is valuable—you must ensure you are absolutely needed at each meeting. Ask someone to brief you afterward, or rely on alternative mediums such as conference calls, Skype, teleseminars, and webinars.

2) **Start on time.** Reward those who arrive on time, and notify the rest that they are wasting everyone's time. Close the door, start on time, and coach latecomers after the meeting. Hint: meetings scheduled for fifteen minutes after the hour have been proven to get better on-time attendance. Try it!

3) **Drop twenty percent.** Could your meetings become shorter just by scheduling them for less time? The Parkinson Principle states that work expands to fit the time allotted. In other words, a one-hour meeting will mysteriously tend to wrap up after around fifty-five minutes, while a ninety-minute meeting will drag on until eighty minutes have passed. The speed with which the meeting progresses is often predicated by the scheduled end time (just think how much more small talk happens at the start of a typical two-hour meeting, compared to a half-hour meeting).

   Instead of scheduling a one-hour meeting, make it for forty-five minutes, and get a commitment from everyone to start on time and stay on task. You may be surprised how this improves the meeting and the results that follow.

Copyright 2003 by Randy Glasbergen.
www.glasbergen.com

GLASBERGEN

"I'm sorry, but I have to move this afternoon's meeting back to yesterday morning. Is that good for you?"

The 16 oz Rule

I love the suggestion from Caterina Fake, co-founder of the popular photo-sharing site, www.flickr.com. As her company grew, Caterina became concerned about excessive meeting time for staff, so she instituted the '16 oz Rule'.[11] "At the beginning of the meeting, everyone has to drink a full glass of water," she explained. "Then we would get very focused and work through the agenda, making as many decisions as possible. But as soon as the first person had to go to the bathroom, the meeting would be over." That's what I call pressure to perform!

---

11. She also subscribes to Jeff Besos's (founder of www.amazon.com) two-pizza rule: project teams should be small enough to feed with two pizzas.

4) **Have meeting agreements.** One of the simplest improvements is an agreement for how the meeting will be managed. Have your committee or team create, and commit to, their own set of agreements. The agreements become the measurement of a successful meeting, and can be used to get a meeting back on track. Here are some sample meeting agreements:

- We will start on time.

- We will respect the speaker. We will let people finish their thoughts, and respect what they shared, before we introduce our own ideas.

- If we miss part of a meeting, it is our responsibility to catch up.

- We will follow our meeting objectives and agenda.

- Presenters will make every effort to arrive early and to come prepared.

- We will stay on topic.

- We will not tolerate personal attacks.

- We will direct our conversation toward consensus-based decisions.

- We will not discuss people who are not present.

- We will end on time, or earlier.

5) **Lead with objectives.** Agendas are useless without objectives. Typical agendas give a chronology of events, such as: "The VP will open the meeting with a welcome," or "Bob will provide an update on the current export plan."

   This is good stuff, but more important is *what we are meeting about* and what we hope to accomplish. Meeting objectives should announce the true purpose of the meeting, provide focus for the discussions, and give the chairperson the boundaries needed to bring a meeting back on track.

Even if you are not using agendas, you should still have a short list of objectives for every meeting (it's okay if they are only announced verbally). At the end of every meeting, allow five to ten minutes to review the objectives, recognize your progress, and confirm who is doing what.

6) **Send homework in advance.** Distribute material, and encourage participants to do their reading *before* the meeting. Homework can include past meeting minutes, a relevant (short) article, or even a couple of provocative questions about the subject. I use these techniques whenever I am preparing for a brainstorming or strategic planning session.[12]

7) **Use a "parking lot."** In the language of facilitation, a "parking lot" is a record of topics, ideas, or concerns that are not on the agenda but need further discussion. Before the meeting ends, ensure that there is a plan for how these items will be handled. This is an excellent way to keep the energy in the meeting focused on objectives and moving forward.

> "A meeting is an event where minutes are taken and hours wasted."
>
> –JAMES T. KIRK, captain of the USS Enterprise

8) **Get ramblers back on track.** Some people love the sound of their own voice. Unfortunately, people who go off-topic or ramble on about their favorite subject can distract other delegates and waste precious time. Having experienced this far too many times, I've created

---

12. I will often have the team complete a short online survey to learn more about their challenges and aspirations. This information is a great starting point for a productive meeting and allows for anonymous comments.

a simple, four-step process that hundreds of my clients now use to deal with unwanted ramblers. The next time you hear, "Oh, that reminds me of the war . . . ," use these four steps to respectfully get the meeting back on track:

1) **Interrupt** – Politely interrupt and get the rambler's attention. You might interrupt with, "Excuse me, John. Let me see if I can summarize what you are saying." Most people will be quite happy if you interrupt and the attention is still on what they were talking about.

2) **Summarize** – Repeat a few key points from what the person said (mentioning only what was related to the topic at hand). "John, it seems you are saying that we also need to consider the history of the association before making a decision."

3) **Confirm** – Show respect for the ideas by asking if your summary is accurate. ". . . Have I got that right?"

4) **Move on** – Turn the attention to someone else, by asking for another opinion, or bringing the group attention back to the meeting objectives. "Who else has an opinion on how we should progress from here?"

9) **Monitor and debrief.** Periodically, ask a volunteer to monitor meeting quality. During the meeting, the monitor makes notes (both positive and negative) about the quality of the meeting. At the end of the meeting, they report back to the group. Great feedback might include:

- Did we stay on track with our objectives?

- Did we keep our comments brief?

- Did we start and end on time?

- Were presenters prepared?

- Did we reach valuable conclusions with accountabilities?

Select one area of development, and commit as a team to work on it at subsequent meetings. You should enjoy at least two wins from this technique: your team will improve in at least one specific area, and your team members will be more aware of their behavior at future meetings.

10) **Plus/Delta your meetings.** Every six meetings or so, there should be a meeting about the meetings. I use a "Plus/Delta" process for these debriefs. Draw a line down the middle of a flip chart. On the left-hand side, under the heading '+', have the group make a list of things that are working or that have improved in recent meetings. On the right-hand side, under the heading 'Δ' (the Greek letter used to symbolize change), make a list of what is not working or could be better.

Once you have your lists, go to the right-hand column and identify a short list of improvements the group can commit to right away. Narrow the list down to a few realistic improvements that can be made relatively soon. Now start a conversation about how to make those changes happen.

Not only will you improve the quality of the meetings in the future, this is also an excellent team builder. Your group will feel heard, more understood, and respected for their opinions, and will (hopefully) welcome the changes.

Standing Room Only

Walk up the single flight of stairs from the main lobby and enter the swinging glass doors and you might think you were observing a well-oiled service machine. People were in their places, phones were being attended to, and you would be greeted at the long front counter promptly. But, like an animal with a terminal illness, first impressions can be deceiving.

This small team was suffering; trust was low, as was morale, and a frustratingly lack of healthy communication was making it difficult for improvements to happen. My job was to help this team to heal and improve morale.

When I got involved, I noticed that staff meetings were infrequent and, when they did occur, were ineffective at best. Lack of information can often lead to distrust and miscommunications. So I decided to start with their meetings.

The following Monday, the team was instructed to convene in their staff room for a meeting, but nobody was allowed to sit. I knew that instituting a regime of morning meetings was destined to fail, unless I could make it easy for them to maintain it. The meetings would start at 8:05 am (twenty-five minutes before the doors open to the public) and would last no longer than ten minutes. Instead of an agenda, the purpose of the meeting was to have a quick check-in and then to share what work needed to be done that day.

It was a communication compromise; a full staff meeting with agendas and objectives would have been ideal, but the need to serve customers made that impractical. All I wanted was for them to practice communicating frequently with each other as a group.

Like the ritual of family meals making for healthy families, we started to notice a difference. There were fewer emails between staff, they started to discuss common work challenges more often, and sick time dropped dramatically. The moral is: when you don't have time to sit, stand!

11) **Make decisions.** An 80% solution is often better than no solution, or revisiting the same discussion every meeting. Set a time limit for your discussion, and agree that you will reach a decision. If you are encountering a stalemate, you can assign a small research project to one person, and postpone the decision until you get new information.

Also, conclude every meeting by having each person announce their new commitments. It quickly becomes obvious when there is no deadline, deliverables are vague, or when someone has taken on too much and will need help.

12) **Finish early.** Whenever you can, wrap up the meeting early. It rewards people for starting on time and staying focused and lets them get back to work early.

What if my Boss is the Problem?

It's not uncommon for the boss—who also chairs the team meetings—to be a part of the problem. Some common issues include: the chair (the boss) commandeers the meeting and doesn't let others speak; the chair rambles on about unrelated topics; or the chair is late to the meeting, or forgets altogether. Left to their own devices, it's unlikely change will happen.

Here's the bottom line: you all want the same thing. Everybody wants the team to succeed. And effective meetings are a part of that success. From that point, you need to get buy-in from the boss to hold a meeting about meetings. (See tip #10, "Plus/Delta your meetings.")

A couple of facilitation notes: It's usually best if the chairperson is not facilitating this meeting. Let someone neutral do that. Start by restating your common objectives. Keep the conversation focused on improving the future, not on dwelling on who did what in the past. And always reach decisions that describe actionable, measurable change.

Meetings are a mixed blessing. They are great for creating dialogue and consensus, but they use up precious time. To start putting your meetings on a diet, try out one of these ideas for a month and notice the difference. Pay attention to attendance (Are people showing up on time?) and results (Were clear decisions made, and are there clear accountabilities and shared responsibility?); these are good measures of healthy meetings.

Meetings Worksheet

Putting meetings on a diet is a system improvement. A little attention and effort in this direction will be good for you and for your team in the long term. You can make individual changes (be on time, be better prepared, etc.) or group changes. This worksheet will help make your meetings leaner and help you arrive at better results.

Changes I can make immediately to the way I attend meetings are:

....

....

....

Changes that we can make, as a team, to enhance our meetings are:

....

....

....

....

....

In the next week, I commit to:

....

....

....

....

....

....

4

• • •

Exorcise Your Email

I don't believe in email. I'm an old-fashioned girl.
I prefer calling and hanging up.

—SARAH JESSICA PARKER, actress

To: jschultz@gofarcom.com
From: tmurray@gofarcom.com
Subject: re: email etiquette
Jeff,

Hope you're well and enjoying the new committee work☺ I'm swamped this week and can't wait for that (long promised) CRM improvement to get going so I can stop the double entries for new contacts.

Anyhow, I need some help from you about email etiquette. I'm hearing from lots of folks that their Inbox is always full and mostly it is internal mail!☺ How about you? Same thing? So, here's what I'm thinking.

Lots of companies have some kind of email etiquette protocol to stop this sort of thing getting out of hand. But I know some folks are in love with their email and there could be resistance to this sort of thing. Remember what happened with the roll out of our values two years ago? It took months to get the buy-in and to work through the edits.

On the other hand I've heard from enough people on the other side of the fence to think it's worth trying to change the way people are using their email now.

Great to get your comments on this.

Cheers

Tim

PS. I know you're swamped, so don't drop everything for this☺

*   *   *

To: tmurray@gofarcom.com
From: jschultz@gofarcom.com
Subject: re: email etiquette
Hey Tim

Great topic! Okay, I know this is an issue for lots of folks. Some will defend their actions (CYA is always there☺). I was also thinking that something formal, across the company would be best. I don't know where to start . . .

What are your ideas for etiquette?

J

*   *   *

To: jschultz@gofarcom.com
From: tmurray@gofarcom.com
Subject: re: email etiquette

Hey thanks Jeff for the response. It's great to be able to get a conversation going about this.

Here's what I'm thinking: we should get others involved through a committee. We need buy-in. And we should collect some data on what's going on out there in email-land. Who's emailing whom, volume of emails received, etc.

T

*   *   *

To: tmurray@gofarcom.com
From: jschultz@gofarcom.com
Subject: re: email etiquette

Yeah, but who's going to have the time for that? I know I'm way overdue on some major projects. Maybe we should start with something simple like an online survey. What do you think?

Jeff

*   *   *

To: jschultz@gofarcom.com
From: tmurray@gofarcom.com
Subject: re: email etiquette

Could work. Where do we start with that? I know Dave has done these before—we could ask him.

T

*   *   *

To: tmurray@gofarcom.com
From: jschultz@gofarcom.com
Subject: re: email etiquette

Good one. Let's follow up on this.

J

*   *   *

If you were counting, that was 360 words in six emails and a whole lot of inaction—especially for two guys who work twenty feet from each other!

Here are three words about email: email is evil.

Well, maybe evil is a bit strong, but let's face it—email is a mixed blessing. No question, it's a cool invention: it's quick, convenient, recorded, searchable, and easy to use. And it wastes hundreds of hours of your time every year, often with little gain to show for your frantic flurry of keyboard pecking.

I've talked to literally thousands of people about their email strife and I think I can safely summarize the source of their email woes in three points:

1) **Email is cheap and easy.** For marketers, email is the Holy Grail of shotgun marketing (what we used to call the spray-and-pray strategy for advertising). The cost is incredibly low, if you don't mind bothering a few hundred people to reach thousands more. According to Forrester Research, the number of marketing emails sent by retailers and wholesalers in the United States hit 158 billion in 2008, and is expected to grow to 258 billion by 2013. More than one-quarter of the email that consumers currently receive in their Inboxes is marketing-related.

   At the same time, email has become the de facto internal communication channel, for quick updates from the committee chair, to invitations for lunch from a buddy ten feet down the hall. The propensity for emailing about everything to everyone has exacerbated the bulging Inbox problem, from an average of 142 emails received per person per day in 2007, to 199 in 2010, and the volume is projected to reach 228 emails per person per day in 2011. It is already estimated that workers are spending between 20 and 40% of their time on email management.[13]

2) **Email all looks the same.** Okay, you get some clues from the subject line, the sender, and so on, but for the most part we have to constantly make decisions about what to look at, and what to ignore. As a result, we spend precious time weeding through the morass of GRLWBH (Get Rich, Lose Weight, Be Happy) sales pitches to find the emails we actually want to read.

   Of course, there are solutions (and I'm going to give you some below), but we are far from having a perfect solution.

3) **Email is omnipresent.** No longer do phone messages and old-fashioned paper mail stay in the office when we go home. We now bring them with us on our smart phones and laptops.[14]

   Studies by AOL on the use of smart phones found that:

   - Nearly 25% of Internet users said they are most likely to check email upon waking[15]

   - 59% are emailing from portable devices in their pajamas in bed

   - 53% are emailing in the bathroom (which gives a new definition to 'urgent')

   - 37% are checking email while they drive

   - 12% admit to checking email while in church[16]

---

13. Spending on email marketing will grow from $1.2 billion in 2007 to $2.1 billion in 2012. Spending on retention strategies for clients using email will more than double during that period. Jupiter Research, New York.

14. More than seven out of ten employed respondents also said they checked their personal email at work—and nearly one-third said they did so more than three times a day. *AOL/Beta Research Corporation.*

15. *AOL/Beta Research Corporation (June 2008)*

16. *AOL/Beta Research Corporation (June 2007)*

At the same time, we are experiencing a blurring of the lines between being 'offline' (not checking Inboxes, voice mail, etc.) and 'online'. Not only has this addiction to connection and staying busy shown up at work big time, it has crept into our personal life.

My experience is that most people are anchored to their email software but their efficiency hasn't improved, despite an exponential increase in the volume of their new emails. Instead of using more sophisticated techniques, or making better decisions on what to read, they simply pour more time into checking, reading, replying, and being frustrated. Yet, combating a growing email volume by just working faster and longer is a sure recipe for burnout. Even a single strategy, like spending five minutes a week to identify senders that repeatedly plug your Inbox and unsubscribe from their lists, will make a noticeable difference. Yet, according to one study, only 22% of professionals ever bother to unsubscribe from unwanted emails.

If the definition of insanity is doing the same thing over and over, expecting a different result, then this behavior certainly meets the definition.

Email and Pavlov

I remember in the late 1980s, when we got our first facsimile machine. The fax machine would ring, and we would stop what we were doing to run across the room and watch the heat-sensitive paper magically curl out of the machine. It only took a few months to learn that most faxes were unwanted advertisements, and our Pavlovian response came to an end.

Although it's wearing off slowly, email still has some of that novelty attached to it. To see the impact, just watch BlackBerry-toting colleagues, commuters on subways, lunch patrons in restaurants, or travelers in airports incessantly checking their email in the middle of a conversation. Some behavioral tracking studies have found that the average worker was checking his/her email thirty to forty times a day. Is it really that important to respond immediately to your messages? It's no wonder that research from the Universities of Glasgow and Paisley found that one-third of workers experienced stress because of their high email volume.

Email and the Path of Least Resistance

The author Robert Fritz coined the expression "path of least resistance" to describe a universal human tendency, when presented with a choice, to take the easier route. You use the drive-through instead of parking and walking, and you avoid confronting the supplier that missed their deadline because you 'don't want to make a scene'.

Or maybe you've done this. You come home brimming with good intentions, determined to squeeze in a much-needed run. As you head for the closet to fetch your runners, the thought of a quick snack seems appealing, and you happily head to the fridge. It's downhill from there. The run is history and the path of least resistance wins again.

For many people, email is the path of least resistance. Reading, responding to, and filing emails gives them a sense of productivity. It usually requires minimal brainpower, and it's a ready-made, auto-refill excuse for avoiding your Boulders. It's no wonder so many people stay busy checking their emails: they are either in avoidance of harder work (think Boulders), or are uncertain about what to work on next, so emails provide a convenient way to stay busy.

It can seem counter-intuitive at first, but doing less (of the wrong work that keeps you busy) means you can do more (of the right work and be less busy).

Your goal should be to use email as a tool, but not to let it control your day. Remember: "Those who don't have goals are ruled by those who do." If you do not have a clear sense of what is important (your Action Plan), email will always be an attractive distraction.

More Busy-ness?

This is a good time to think about your time goals (remember these from the "Time Management Self-Assessment" on page 19?). What are you saving time for? Will you fill your new-found minutes with more busy-ness? Or are you seeking more time for reflection, organizing, and time with family? Once your objectives are clear and meaningful, distractions, like email, begin to lose their appeal. It's all about clarity of objectives, focus, and staying the course.

What is the Pain?

One of the basic principles of creating lasting change is that we must start with a clear picture of our current reality. It's no different than fixing your car, your health, a relationship, or the balance in your bank account; the more accurate your understanding of what is wrong and what it is costing you, the more motivated you can be to fix it.

Let's start with a quick calculation of the time you are spending on email now.

In the space provided below, record the number of emails you open, read, and respond to in the course of a day (for this exercise, consider that deleting or filing an email counts as a response).

Then make an estimate of the average time you spend per email (e.g.: one and one-half minutes/email). Finally, calculate the total time per year that you spend on email (again, we will use the estimate of 250 days worked per year in our calculation) and divide it by sixty to find the total hours per year (if you want to really get depressed, divide this number by forty to get a total number of weeks per year spent on email).

(a) Average number of emails received per day that you look at: _____

(b) Average time spent on each email: _____

Total time per year = (a) _____ × (b) _____ × 250: _____/60 = _____ hours/year

Here's a typical example:

Total time per year = (a) 35 × (b) 1.5 × 250 = 13,125/60 = 218 hours/year

Total time: 218 hours/year/40 = 5.5 weeks/year!

Imagine what a difference small improvements in your email management systems might make if repeated day after day. If you receive an average of fifty emails every day, and you are able to either reduce your viewing time by ten minutes, or save at least ten seconds per email, you can recover about one full work-week every year.

Now that I have your attention, let's look at solutions . . .

Email Tips and Tricks

The following tips and tricks for quickly reducing time on email are the best I have found, taught, and used myself. Use any one of these techniques, and you could easily be saving as much as half an hour a day (the average for our clients is one hour per day saved). Practice using these techniques for thirty days, and I know you will have more freedom—and people will be coming around to find out your secret.[17]

1) **Check your email less often.** If there is one change that everyone should make, this is it: check your Inbox less frequently. By simply going to your Inbox fewer times, you will have more time to work on your Boulders. You will be able to focus more on completing tasks, and you will feel less frantic at the end of the day.[18] Here is the formula I use:

   - **8:45 am** – After checking my Day and Action Plans, I check email, but only to respond to emergencies, clients, or client-related work that I know was left over from the day before. Total time spent: about fifteen minutes.

   - **10:30 am** – Check email (about thirty minutes).

   - **1:45 pm** – Check email (about fifteen minutes). This is a quick check for returned messages and any important new messages.

   - **3:30 pm** – Check email (about thirty minutes). I spend more time composing longer responses and cleaning up my Inbox.

---

17. Note that these solutions were designed for Outlook 2003 and 2007. Similar solutions are available for later versions of Outlook as well as for Entourage on the Mac.

18. Obviously, if your work depends on being on email all day, that's simply the way it has to be. However, it may be that you have simply developed a habit of constantly checking your email.

The total time taken to check my email is about ninety minutes. I know that this might be much higher than you experience now, but for me, it is about one-half of the time that I was formerly spending on email. The main difference now is that I make my Action Plan my priority.

No Temptations

One of the easiest and most reliable ways to stay off your email and focus on your Boulders is to simply not have Outlook open. As soon as you click 'Exit', you are declaring that this is uninterrupted focus-time and you are working under *your* direction. No pop-ups, no temptations—just set your timer and get to work.

Two things might surprise you: you get a lot done (and you may notice your ability to focus and think has improved), and the emails will wait!

2) **Set Outlook to start with Calendar and Tasks.** Focusing on important appointments and tasks without email distractions is a great way to start your day.[19] Even better, when you boot up in the morning, is to not open Outlook at all. If you are a morning person, this is precious time to protect—avoid the distraction of a blinking Inbox.

3) **Use the right medium.** Like the carpenter who only has a hammer and starts to see everything as a nail, it's easy to fall into the habit of using email for most of your communication.

---

19. Go to *Tools > Options > Other > Advanced Options*. Under *General Settings*, next to the *Startup* button in this folder box, click *Browse* and select *Calendar*.

In recent years, there have been cases of companies announcing staff layoffs by email, or of embarrassing inter-office email correspondence being used as court evidence. Just because you have email and they have email does not mean that this is the best communication medium. Often we are replacing good old-fashioned, face-to-face conversations with email—to our detriment.

Here is a good rule of thumb: if the message involves emotions (attempts to motivate, complaints, or negative comments about other people) or is complex in nature (multi-faceted, requires dialogue, is contentious, etc.), don't hit 'Send'—walk down the hall, or pick up the phone.

4) **Use the subject line creatively.** If you are involved in a series of emails on one topic (like sending out a document for others to review), change the subject line every time you respond. For example "re: agenda for review" becomes "re: agenda for review II." Or "re: agenda for review—HM's comments." Here are two more tips for using the subject line effectively:

- **Create codes** – Simple, agreed-upon abbreviations in the subject line can save time and help reduce email volume. Examples include: NRN = No Response Necessary, and EOM = End Of Message.

- **Change the subject line** – If you receive an email that you know you will need to find later (a quote from a supplier, your airline confirmation, the agenda for a meeting, etc.), simply retype the subject line, resave it, and it's now easier to find next time.

5) **Turn notification of new messages off.** I think that, when this default option was built into email software, the average person must have been receiving ten emails per week. Now, with

the exception of day traders on the stock market or newspaper reporters, most folks will be much better served by visiting their email on *their* schedule, not on that of the sender. If you have notifications turned on for email and/or instant messenger, and were to watch for just one day, I think you would be amazed by the number of distracting notifications you are receiving. Remember, your number one priority at work is to get the highest ROI (Return On Investment) work completed. And these are exactly the kinds of jobs that require the most focused, time-consuming, concentration. Every time your notification pops up on the screen (or worse yet, you hear the notification sound), you are visually and mentally pulled away from your work. This just doesn't make any sense.

Turn your notifications off and you will notice a dramatic difference to your day, right away. Check your email on *your* schedule, not theirs.[20]

6) **Less is best.** When you invest an hour to compose an in-depth dissertation that would make your business professor proud, you've not only created a lot of work for yourself, but for the poor reader as well.

Two strategies that can make email a more useful tool: keep your content brief and your responses even briefer (yes, 'Less is Best' might be a second theme to this book). Remember, it is often faster and simpler to call the person, leave a voice mail message, or arrange a short meeting.

---

20. Go to *Tools > Options > Preferences > Email Options > Advanced Email Options.* Under *"When new items arrive in my Inbox,"* unclick all options.

Improve your typing speed

Okay, I admit this suggestion might not be popular but—trust me—it will be worth it.

Do the math: If you could increase your typing speed by even ten percent, how much time could you be saving every day? The average adult types at about 38–40 words per minute, whereas a professional typist would crank out the words in 70–80 (and some hit warp speed numbers, like 100–110 words per minute). Here are reasons why learning to type faster makes sense:

We all have to type. Other than your phone, which might not allow you to use more than your thumbs to compose a message, you are using your keyboard all day. Even you IT folks, who think you use your mouse more than the keyboard, would do well to actually observe how often you have to send off a quick reply to a customer or compose some copy for an FAQ document.

If you can type faster, you can allocate more brainpower to composition, and less to the mechanics of finding the 'h' when you just hit the 'j' by mistake. This means you will write better, spend less time editing, and produce better results from your writing.

Here's some simple math: Suppose that you type at about 30–40 words per minute now. With just a little bit of practice, you double your speed to sixty words per minute. Now if you were typing for just one hour per day (and many of our clients are typing at least three times this per day), this increase in speed would save you some three weeks a year just in typing time![21]

---

21. A fun way to get started is to Google "free typing test" and see what your current speed is. Make a goal to increase your speed by at least ten percent. If you practice just a few times, you will be amazed at how quickly your speed increases.

7) **Color-code your email.** A simple way to highlight important mail from a client or co-worker is to have Outlook color-code the unread email when it arrives.[22] You can also uniquely color emails sent directly to you (as opposed to being cc'd) so they stand out.

8) **Park emails.** If you receive an email that doesn't need your attention immediately, right-click and drag it to the Tasks bar (bottom left of screen). Now here's the trick: once your mouse pointer is over the destination you want (Calendar, Contacts, or Tasks), release your right-click button on your mouse and a small window will open, giving you four choices (three for Tasks). If you choose one of the *Copy* options, a copy of the email will be created, and the unread email will remain in your Inbox. The *Move* option will create a new Task, and will remove the email from your Inbox.

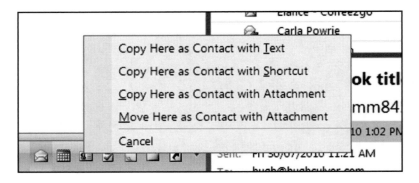

If you are creating a new Task from the email, select the date you need to respond to the email or take action, choose

---

22. Click on an email from that person and go to *Tools > Organize*. Click on the *Using Colors* option on the left. Look for the instruction line, *Color Messages*. Choose *from* [sender], choose a color, and click on *Apply Color*.

the Category the email belongs to, turn the reminder off and—presto!—you have a new task, with a copy of the email in the body of the Task, and a copy left in your Inbox.

Use the same technique to create a calendar entry from an email. Suppose someone sends you a confirmation about the meeting date you talked about, or an announcement for an event you plan to attend. Simply right-click and drag the confirmation email to the Calendar bar (bottom left of your screen). You now have a new Calendar entry, with the content of the email in the text body.

You can also drag the email from a new contact into Contacts, and it will automatically start to build the contact information for you. Often you can Copy/Paste the rest of their contact information from the Notes box into the appropriate content fields.

Note: Once your pointer is hovering over the destination icon (Calendar, Contacts, or Tasks), the trick is to release the right button on your mouse.

9) **Don't open an email until you are ready to deal with it.** Avoid the habit of opening an email, thinking about it, and then marking it 'unread'. This is the twenty-first century version of the sage advice, "Only touch a piece of paper once." All you are doing is delaying the inevitable. When you preview an email, make an immediate decision to reply immediately, delete it, right-click and flag it for future action, forward it, or drag it to Tasks or Calendar (see 'Park emails' above). You will have fewer 'Unreads' staring at you from your Inbox, and will feel—and be—more productive.

10) **Don't repeat yourself.** When responding to emails, do you find that you are often typing the same information over and over again? I found that this happened most often when we received requests for information and details about our seminars and

keynotes, or other upcoming events. I hate retyping something that I have already created, or digging it out of a past email. There is a better way.

When you have created a block of text that you know you could re-use for future emails (standard replies, dates of events, descriptions of services, disclaimers, directions to your office, and so on), highlight them and store them in AutoText, Signatures, or in Office 2007 QuickParts. The next time you need that text, it is right there in your email software, ready to be used.

Reduce, Recycle, Reuse

Here's how to easily reuse email content:

- Click and highlight the text you want to copy, then hit CTRL+C (Control + Copy).
- Click on *Tools > Options.* Click on *Mail Format,* then on *Signatures.* Click on *New,* and enter a name for your new entry. Next, paste the entry with CTRL+V (Control + paste). Finish with *OK > OK.*
- In Office 2007, go to Quick Parts in the Insert menu. You can easily load this up with logos, directions, product descriptions, images, or virtually anything!

There are other techniques as well:

- Once you send the original response email with the text you want to reuse in the future, simply find the email in your 'Sent Items' folder, click and drag it to Drafts, and there it is for future use. Next, open that email, change the Subject Line to something you will easily recognize for future use, click on *Esc* and you will be asked if you want to save changes to this message; click on *Yes*. Note: The next time you want to reuse this message, simply *Forward* the email to a new email address and the original one will stay in Drafts for the next use.

11) Create Folders in Outlook. Imagine not having even a basic filing system in your office—crazy, right? Now look at how you are using your email software. Do you have a filing system for those hundreds of emails you get weekly?

Folders and Rules are two dynamite tools for organizing your Inbox—when set up properly, the software serves as a gatekeeper for all incoming emails. Because the folders are organized by subject or sender, you can instantly prioritize which emails you will read, and which ones can wait until later. *This one idea alone can save you from spending two to five hours a week, needlessly wading through unfiltered emails.*

First, create your folders (right-click on your Inbox and click on *New Folder*). I use folders for client projects, staff, sub-contractors, and suppliers (such as my web design folks). Avoid embedding one folder inside another (in other words, always right click on 'Inbox' when creating new folders). If the main folder is closed, you won't be able to tell if the sub-folder has new emails.

A favorite folder I have created is labeled 'News'—this is for e-zines, newsletters, advertisements, and other group mail-outs I am interested in, but only on my schedule. About once a month, I look at the 300 to 400 emails in 'News', quickly read the ones I'm interested in, and then delete them all. That's 300 to 400 emails that never land in my Inbox, and that I can deal with in less than fifteen minutes, once a month. Nice.

Once you have created your folders, you are ready to create the rules to automatically move the new emails into their folders.[23]

Right-click on a new email that you want to go into a folder. Choose '*Create Rule*', click on the checkbox '*From* [sender]', then click on the checkbox '*Move the item to folder*'. Click on '*Select Folder*' and choose the appropriate folder. Finish with '*OK > OK*'.

A window will appear, asking if you want to run your new rule on all messages in the current folder. Click the checkbox and select '*OK*'.

Once you create a rule for a person, the following one-time change will create a rule that instructs Outlook to store emails both received from and sent to that person in the same folder: Go to **Tools > Options > Preferences > Email Options > Advanced Email Options** *and check* '**In folders other than the Inbox, save replies with original message**'.

Once you have these folders set up, you need to get in the habit of checking folders first. When you open Outlook, look for folders that are 'lit up' with a blue number beside them (indicating the number of emails unread). Based on the relative importance of the folders, decide which ones to read first and which ones to ignore.

My typical routine is to read email in client folders, then office folders, then project folders, in that order. Only then will I scan recent additions to my Inbox. This puts new emails on *my schedule,* not on that of the sender.

---

23. If you want to change the order of your folders, simply right-click and rename a folder to move it higher or lower, alphabetically.

Learn Shortcut Keys

Shortcut keys can cut your time on email by another ten percent. With shortcut keys taking you straight to the action you want, you avoid having to search for the pull-down menus. You will notice that most shortcut keys are combinations found in the lower left-hand corner of the keyboard. This means that you can be using the mouse with your right hand while moving quickly to where you want to go with the other hand. If you want to start using shortcuts, print out this list of popular shortcuts (for Windows-based computers) and keep it by your keyboard for a month.

CTRL+SHIFT+K (create a new task in Outlook)
CTRL+SHIFT+M (create a new email message in Outlook)
CTRL+SHIFT+C (add new contact in Outlook)
CTRL+SHIFT+A (add new appointment in Outlook)

To negotiate emails faster, practice these shortcuts:

CTRL+F (forward)
CTRL+R (reply to Sender)
CTRL+SHIFT+R (reply to All)
ALT+S (Send)

These are universal Microsoft edit shortcuts:

CTRL+Z (undo)	CTRL+N (new doc)
CTRL+C (copy)	CTRL+O (open doc)
CTRL+V (paste)	CTRL+W (close doc)
CTRL+X (delete)	CTRL+S (save doc)
CTRL+B (bold)	CTRL+P (print doc)

12) The One Month test. Still stuck with a couple of hundred emails in your Inbox? I like to put these to the 'One Month' test. Here's how: create a new folder in your Inbox, titled 'One Month Hold [date]' (enter the date one month from now).

Next, change your view to show only unread emails, by selecting *View > Current View > Unread Messages in This Folder*. Select all emails that show up as unread (CTRL+A). Then click and drag all selected emails to your new folder. Change your view back to show all emails (*View > Current View > Messages*). And, voila!—you have parked your unread emails out of sight. The date on the folder will let you know when to revisit the content (you can also create a flag with a bring-forward date).

I wait for one month, and then either just delete the whole folder, or quickly scan for any emails that need a response. It is amazing how few emails I find that actually need a response. Besides, if it's really important, someone will usually remind me or resend the message.

Creating a Team Solution

I've just provided the best solutions for reducing your time on email, but what about a team approach? More and more, I am hearing of team-wide or corporate-wide approaches to reducing time spent on email. In my opinion, this is a 'must-do' for any group that is experiencing anything more than minor time inconvenience from email volume.

Getting together to explore strategies that everyone can benefit from will not only give folks permission to change their ways, it will also raise awareness about what is acceptable practice, and what is not.

One of the first corporate-wide email solutions I read about was from Pfizer Canada. As an experiment, vice-president Jon Coleman sent out an email to ten direct reports at 10:00 am on a Sunday morning, requesting some feedback on a client issue. Within one hour, eight people had responded. He was shocked by this 'always on' attitude. "Many people judge their productivity based on how many emails they've responded to," said Coleman. "That's a ridiculous measure."[24]

The new Pfizer policy, called 'Freedom six to six', bans email between 6 pm and 6 am and on weekends. The company also brought in trainers, to teach staff how to be efficient with email.

Other team or organization-based solutions could be to:

- Provide training. I'm constantly amazed at how few people have taken the time to learn even the basics, such as shortcut keys, folders, signatures, search, or attachments.

- Have Blackout Fridays, when no emails are sent or read.

- Forward all enterprise-wide status reports and announcements to RSS subscriptions.

- Use 'No Reply Needed' (or 'NRN') in the subject field. This will help cut down on those "thank you/you're welcome" emails that gum up your Inbox.

- Establish some agreements on email etiquette, covering topics such as: appropriate email use (don't use email for conflict resolution or talking about the boss); professionalism; protection from liability; use of attachments; proofreading; copy vs. blind copy (cc vs. bcc); and use of priority flags.

- Have a "Quiet Time"—a block of the day when email and IM (Instant Messaging) notifications are turned off, and email is checked once every hour instead.

---

24. http://www.macleans.ca/business/companies/article.jsp?content=20060130_120699
    _120699

- Post staff newsletters on an intranet site, instead of using email for distribution.

- Provide free typing lessons (really!). Hey, I know I'm harping on this, but doesn't it make sense? If you are paying someone $60,000 plus bonuses, that's about $1 per minute. Don't you think a $20 investment to download a typing lesson is worth it?

Ban Excessive CC'ing

If Mary was working on a document and wanted to have seven colleagues offer editing comments, she could email all of them. No problem so far. But what if everyone on that list decided to share their comments, edits, and thoughts with the whole group, by using 'Reply All'? Obviously, that would generate seven times seven, or forty-nine, responses. To continue with this scenario, if Mary was then to take their suggestions, make changes to the document, and re-circulate it for comments two more times, and if each time, 'Reply All' was used by all respondents, the total number of emails generated could be as much as 168, depending on how many replied.[25]

Take this simple scenario and extrapolate it across the whole company, and you can have a tsunami of pointless replies and cc'ing generated between staff.

Of course, using 'Reply All' or cc'ing extra people is not done with mal intent (or is it?). People often just want to keep others informed, or seek their input. The downside, however, is more email volume. And when Inboxes are already full, being cc'd by a colleague on something you really don't need to know becomes more of an irritation than a benefit.

A friend who teaches at a university often complains that internal

---

25. The original three emails from Mary, times seven, plus three times forty-nine.

email is so riddled with unwanted barbeque announcements and unrelated staff policy updates, he rarely reads any of it. If these tedious, 'nice-to-know' emails are filling his Inbox, imagine the impact across the whole campus.

I recommend that you start with your own practices, and become more aware of when, and when not, to 'cc:' others. Next, get senior staff to support this policy. Third, create some simple, protocol to direct email usage. For example, one client will address group emails using blind carbon copy (bcc:) and copy the email addresses into the body of the message. This way, people receiving the email know who else received it, but can't easily reply to all recipients.

Go to the Source

One of the simplest solutions is to go to the source, and look at why staff are sending so many emails. As an exercise, go through an average day's email, and group them into categories: client-related, committee/team, staff, boss, etc. Then ask: which groups are using email excessively, and how can you reduce this?

For most organizations, the 'need-to-know' and 'nice-to-know' chatter are obvious culprits. Just one meeting with your team about this could be the start of a dramatic reduction of lost time.

For any kind of team development process, I always like to start by recognizing what is working (use your Plus/Delta technique—see page 109). Ask the group for a list of what is going well with team communications, including electronic communications. Make this list in the left-hand column. Don't stop until you have a healthy record of what is working well.

Next, ask the group for a list of what could be improved. Record everything—even if the suggestion seems unrealistic (e.g. email-free Fridays), record it. Once you have a good list, have the team rate the suggestions in terms of being realistic and valuable. Finally, create a plan to turn one or two of the top choices into action.

When I used this process with a team recently, it was exciting to see the ideas flying onto the flip chart. After only ten minutes, we had a list of changes that included: posting meeting minutes on the company Intranet for later retrieval; having a one-page email length rule; agreeing to include a necessary action in every email; and not to send emails to colleagues after 12:00 noon on Fridays.

Encourage Human Moments

John works in a forestry department and relies heavily on email to communicate with colleagues, many of whom are either in the field or at remote offices. One day he was working on a report that was due that week, and needed some current statistics from a colleague. So he did what most of us would do: he sent an email request.

One day passed without a response, so he again sent an email, with the same request. The next day, with his frustration increasing, he sent a second reminder email—this time with the 'Urgent' flag. Still, no response.

Finally, on the third day, completely perplexed and frustrated, John stood up, leaned over the cubicle wall, and said, "Can I please have those statistics!?!"

Sometimes we just need to get off our butts, walk down the hall, and connect.

Edward Hallowell, author of *CrazyBusy,* calls for more of what he terms "human moments" in the workplace. These are the moments when people actually meet, and talk face-to-face. "I believe that it has started to disappear from modern life," says Hallowell, "and I sense that we all may be about to discover the destructive power of its absence."[26]

He warns that our addiction to electronic communications (cell

---

26. Hallowell likens some symptoms he sees in the workplace as being similar to Attention Deficit Disorder in adults.

phone, email, conference calls, Skype, voice mail, etc.) lessens the quality of communications, and is a negative contributor to social and individual health in the workplace.

Meet with your team, start a conversation about electronic vs. human moments, and create agreements on simple strategies that will allow more of the latter and less of the former. You might be surprised to discover how many other people are experiencing the same frustrations and anxiety about these issues.

A Word about Social Media

It has only been a few years since Facebook, MySpace, Twitter, LinkedIn, and the growing family of social media sites started their exponential growth onto the Broadband and into our lives. What was once a novelty is now considered as normal as using the telephone (or more normal, for many). According to Facebook's own statistics, one-half of their over 500 million users log on every day, with the average user spending fifty-five minutes there—every day. According to the Radicati Group, this shows up as eight percent of their workday, or thirty-eight minutes. According to a separate study, some corporations are finding that as much as 12% of their company's Internet bandwidth is being gobbled up by use of social media sites.

Whether you are sneaking a post to friends or twittering about your great sandwich at lunch, time on social media sites at work is obviously wrong (unless, of course, that is your job). And if you are an entrepreneur, you should really question the volume of time you spend in this arena without a clear plan on how it will benefit your business.

I still blog and enjoy the conversations that get started there. And I send out tweets, but only to let people know about some of my recent posts, upcoming events, or free materials I'm offering. But check with me in a year—I'm sure the social media scene will have all changed by then—and so will my thoughts on how to use it.

Email Worksheet

To reduce my time on email and to have more control over how my email is processed, I will:

....

....

....

The one-time changes I will make (set up folders, turn off the notification for new emails, etc.) are:

....

....

....

....

....

....

The new habits I will adopt (stop checking email throughout the day, use shortcut keys, etc.) are:

....

....

....

....

....

....

....

5

● ● ●

Clearing the Clutter

For the first twenty-five years of my life, I wanted freedom.
For the next twenty-five years, I wanted order.
For the next twenty-five years, I realized that order is freedom.

—WINSTON CHURCHILL, British politician

The last of the four large recycling bins was being rolled down the hall, and the end was in sight. It had taken a total of twelve hours over the last two weeks, and Jerrod had seen enough planning documents, rolled maps, and consulting reports to last a lifetime. He was tired and his back ached, but he felt a growing enthusiasm as he looked around him.

Two weeks earlier, his office had been the joke of the floor. The stacks of disorganized reports and papers had been piled high on every conceivable flat space. Maneuvering a body within the confines of this fifth-floor office took a gymnast's skills, and nothing seemed to have an order or a system. And yet it had been Jarrod's home for eight hours a day, five days a week, for the last eight years.

After today, however, things were going to be different. As an assignment for a leadership program I was instructing, Jarrod had chosen to clear the clutter from his office. The benefits he would enjoy will go far beyond just being able to find the paper he is looking for. In Jarrod's own assessment, "This will add years to my life."

Workspace clutter is a silent killer of effective work and healthy mental attention. Clutter distracts you, confuses your thinking, exhausts your work capacity, and sets a poor example for others.

Everyone who takes this advice is surprised by the positive effect it has on their work, their attitude, and even their health. It can, however, be one of the hardest changes to make, and to stick with. So first, let me convince you why it's worth the effort.

In a study of 800 Hewlett-Packard employees (conducted by cognitive neuropsychologist Dr. David Lewis), half the group was asked to work in an overcrowded and disorderly work environment, while the second half worked in an area that was open and bright. While neither group thought their situation was unusual, either in terms of being able to get work done or getting interrupted, that is where the similarity ended.

On every measure, the second group outperformed their counterparts; and the differences in performance were nothing short of extraordinary. Productivity was up 400%, stress levels were down 50%, and IQ scores went up 28%. In addition, blood pressure went down, short-term memory improved, and participants retained 33% more information.

The conclusion: clutter and disorganization are silent barriers to our success that dramatically impact our health.

Continuous Partial Attention

Ex-Apple executive, Linda Stone, has turned her attention from growing world leadership in technology to writing about the impact of this same technology on humans. In 1998, she theorized that our constant multi-tasking was actually impacting our ability to focus, converse, and make decisions. She coined the expression "Continuous Partial Attention" (CPA).[27] As we are motivated by our desire to do more and to be more efficient, "CPA lets you cast a wider net," but the downside, she explains, is that "it also runs the risk of keeping you from really studying the fish."

Nicholas Carr goes one evolutionary step further in his book, *The Shallows*, and presents a convincing (and somewhat scary) argument that our mind is already being altered by our intense use of the Internet and all of its multifarious services.[28] He argues that, just as previous 'tools of the mind', like the clock, printing press, and maps, changed how we process information, the Internet is no different. And while we are more adept at "rapid, distracted sampling of small bits of information from many sources," we are losing our capacity for concentration, contemplation, and reflection.

While there is no turning back time, it is always possible to turn back the speed of life, and to make time for simple conversations, downtime, and single-tasking.

In addition to distracting us from what we are working on, interruptions can come with a mental cost. In a rather unique comparison study, psychiatrist Glenn Wilson, at King's College in London, found that, when juggling email interruptions at the same time as the rest of their work, the IQ of office workers fell by a "shocking" ten points. This drop is the equivalent of missing a night's sleep, or

---

27. http://lindastone.net/qa/continuous-partial-attention/
28. Nicholas Carr, *The Shallows: What the Internet Is Doing to Our Brains*, W. W. Norton & Company, 2010.

more than double the mean drop found in pot smokers! "We have found that this obsession with looking at messages, if unchecked, will damage a worker's performance by reducing their mental sharpness," Wilson reports. "This is a very real and widespread phenomenon."[29]

When you have clutter on your desk, on the floor, around your computer monitor, or on your brain, you force your thinking process to attempt to multi-task. Here's my rule of thumb: If you can see or are aware of unfinished work, your brain will think about it. *This covers everything from a report you are working on to the unreturned pink phone slips or the sticky note reminding you of some login password. If you are thinking about it (even for a moment) while trying to work on something else, you are multi-tasking. Like a juggler trying to keep his plates from crashing to the floor, this synapse leaping from one distraction to another, and then another, is exhausting. We may do it because we can, but we're simply not designed for it—no one is.*

The Temptation to Multi-Task

Bear with me as I give you a scenario that you might recognize:

You've just arrived at your desk for the day, and have started to work on your emails. With a fresh cup of coffee and your plan updated, you feel confident and determined to get lots of work done today.

After looking at about six emails and responding to two or three, you see one that refers to a file you worked on earlier that year. The

---

29. MacLean's Magazine, Jan., 2006.

answer you need is in the file, so you get up and head to the other room to fetch the file.

Once there, a vague feeling of uncertainty washes over you, and you realize that you are at a sudden loss as to why you are in this room (I'm sure this won't make any sense to you readers under the age of fifty). "Ah, yes!" you exclaim to yourself, "the file—that's why I'm here." Slightly reassured, you return to your desk to continue your response to the email.

No sooner do you sit down than the phone rings. Another department is calling, to ask for changes to a report you are working on. Slightly frustrated, and with one eye on the new-found file and your email, you make notes about the call on a note pad.

Already you are feeling frustrated. Your Day Plan is becoming derailed, your desk is accumulating piles of partially finished work, and your computer screen is decorated with sticky reminders for the day.

The call finished, you notice two phone message slips from yesterday and a brochure for an upcoming industry conference you are considering attending.

Determined to complete something, you start to read the brochure and circle workshops that look interesting. Only two minutes into this new task, you notice a small pile of business cards you brought back from the last client presentation. One of the cards is from a vendor you are interested in, and who you promised to follow up with. You pick it up and decide to have a quick look at the vendor's website, to see if the product pricing is listed. After a fruitless eight minutes on the website, you remember the client's email that you were already working on. You turn back to the original email, but notice a new email from your boss that might need immediate attention.

You open it to look, realize it can wait (so you mark it 'Unread'), and decide to have a quick peek at the website of the conference you were just looking at. Just then, Anne-Marie sticks her head in the doorway and asks: "Have you got a minute?" Arrggh!

Does this sound familiar? Your attention is scattered between multitudes of unrelated tasks, more attention-grabbing distractions are coming in every few minutes, and you feel like you are spinning your wheels, but going nowhere.

Here's a quick quiz: In the scenario above, how many subjects or items are now open in your brain? Three? Five? Seven? Nine? The correct answer is at least nine. According to George Miller's classic 1960s studies at Harvard, you have a thinking capacity of about seven items, plus or minus two.[30] This means that, with nine items on your mind, your mental RAM is beyond capacity.[31] No wonder you feel frustrated if the phone rings or someone drops in for advice!

Multi-tasking, or the attempt to deal with a number of tasks at once, is not only inefficient—it typically leads to increased stress levels, a greater chance of making mistakes, and a general feeling of being overwhelmed. As Hallowell warns, "It may be convenient or necessary to multi-task, to talk on the telephone as you write

---

30. This research completed at Harvard was coined the "magic number seven, plus or minus two," and was apparently influential in the origin of the seven-digit phone numbers created by AT&T.

31. Sorry for the computer jargon: RAM stands for Random-Access Memory and provides a great analogy for the cerebral capacity we have. There's lots of capacity until you start opening a lot of software, or in our case, start thinking about loads of projects, people, and potential problems.

an email and watch the stock prices stream across your computer screen; or to put clothes in the dryer as you play with your toddler and talk to your real estate agent on the phone. However, you will not be doing any of those tasks as effectively as you would if you were doing them one at a time."

You might be surprised to learn that your attempts to complete a number of tasks all at once are actually doing you a great disservice. "As it turns out," states an article in *Scientific American Mind* magazine, "the human brain cannot truly ape the computer's knack of crunching data in the background while toggling among processing windows . . . trying to juggle various jobs, rather than completing them sequentially, can take longer overall and leave the multi-taskers with a reduced ability to perform each task."[32]

With our increased use of computers, social networking sites and smart phones, and wider access to the Internet at work, at home, and wherever we travel, the temptation to multi-task has never been greater. We can always be connected, and conversations follow us electronically and wait to fill all our available minutes. Yet there is a growing resistance to the 'always on' lifestyle.

A study by Families and Work Institute in New York City found that some 45% of US workers believe they are asked, or expected, to work on too many tasks at once. And in a study by the US National Association of Professional Organizers, 91% of workers say they'd be more efficient if their workspace was better organized. More than a quarter said they would save more than an hour a day by being more organized at work.

---

32. Scientific American Mind magazine, January 2005.

Generation X is No Better

It turns out that members of the X-Box generation, although terrific at shooting down space aliens while focusing on five other things, haven't been developing valuable skills for the workplace (unless of course, their work involves shooting down space aliens).

A study at Stanford University found that Generation Xers (the first true high-tech age cohort, born between 1961 and 1981), are chronic media multi-taskers who actually have difficulty focusing, and are unable to ignore irrelevant information. "We knew that multi-tasking was difficult from a cognitive perspective," Stanford symbolic systems professor Eyal Ophir said. "We thought, 'What's this special ability that people have that allows them to multi-task?' Rather than finding things that they were doing better, we found things they were doing worse."[33] The surprise is that multi-tasking at high speed on video games doesn't seem to lead to skills for focused attention to detail or for deliberating on a single, important decision. Strike one for the Boomers!

Researchers also believe that the stress associated with multi-tasking may contribute to short-term memory difficulties. In short, multi-tasking can result in inefficiency, sloppy thinking, and mistakes. Isn't it bizarre that firms still place help-wanted ads listing "ability to multi-task" as a desirable skill? Perhaps I have convinced you of the negative side effects of physically attempting to do multiple activities at once, but what about mental multi-tasking?

---

33. "Multi-taskers of media 'lousy' at everything," by Clare Baldwin. For more information on this study, go to http://news.stanford.edu/pr/2009/multitask-research-release-082409. html Calgary Herald, August 25, 2009.

Mental Distraction in a Box

When we moved into our new office a few years ago and finished unpacking, I noticed one banker's box on the floor unopened. "No problem," I told myself. "I'll get to it when I have a few minutes."

Every time I got up for a cup of tea or to meet with staff, I'd spot that orphan box, and remind myself of my promise: "Someday I'm going to take a few minutes and empty that box." Over and over again throughout the day and the week, this became my mantra.

Ten months of mental nagging later, the box was still there—an icon of cardboard-clad guilt. Every time I glanced over at the box, another anchor for my procrastination was dropped into my subconscious. This was not the kind of programming I needed, and I certainly didn't need the mental distraction!

Finally, one Friday as I was about to head home, I stopped in front of the dreaded box and opened the lid. Out of sheer frustration, I decided to put an end to this distraction routine. And I started going through the contents. Nothing! There was literally *nothing* of value in the box.

Most of the contents went into recycling.

I haven't done the math, but my guess is that, over those ten months, I must have thought about that box, even if for just a passing moment, some half-dozen times a day. That's over 1,000 mental detours that were completely unnecessary and that only took seven minutes to resolve.

Not convinced? There is a brilliant self-test created over half a century ago by John Ridley Stroop, a professor of psychology, that should get your attention and prove that multi-tasking slows your computation time and distracts your thinking.

Here is a mini-version of the Stroop test to whet your appetite.[34]

---

34. I have posted a larger, color version of this test at www.hughculver.com/break book.

In this exercise, you simply have to concentrate on saying to yourself the color of the letters (don't read the word). For example, for the first one you would say 'black', and so on.

Did you notice how difficult and slow it is to try to process the two bits of information: the color of the font and (although you were not asked to) the word itself?

Next time you are working on a report or project that requires all of your concentration, try this—turn on a radio station with music that you don't like, and notice what happens to your concentration. You might be one of those rare people who can be completely oblivious to external noise distractions. I know I'm certainly not.

It's no wonder we are seeing a growing ban on the use of cell phones while driving. Anyone who has tried dialling or texting while behind the wheel has experienced how quickly our cognitive abilities are hijacked by even the slightest attempts to multi-task.

Now I want you to consider your workspace. Take a moment to visualize the desk that you spend so many hours at, or if you are at your desk, stand up, step back five feet, and actually take it in:

1) How organized is your desk and the area around it?

2) Do you see papers that haven't been touched for months? (Moving them around on your desk doesn't count.)

3) Are there files on the floor, or on top of filing cabinets, that are collecting dust?

4) Are there sticky notes surrounding your computer monitor competing for your attention?

I have become convinced that getting my workspace organized and keeping it that way is one of the simplest, and most powerful ways for me to stay focused and be more effective. But it does require ongoing attention—gravity has a nasty way of defying your best efforts.

If you think you need to clean up your act and stop multi-tasking, here are some quick remedies that will lead to better performance and less stress.

The Five-Minute Purge

Here's where you need to start. Take five minutes at the end of every day to put paperwork in its place. Your goal should be to remove from sight anything that will draw your attention away from the immediate task (this includes sticky notes, telephone messages, brochures, and anything that no longer belongs on your desk).

Start by recycling brochures, trade magazines, and that article someone suggested you read two months ago. Make a decision to toss them all into recycling. Trust me, if anything is really important, someone will let you know (I doubt that will happen, though—they are all too busy going through the papers on their own desks).

Next, consider your filing systems. Put any files or notes that belong in filing cabinets in their place. You will end up with papers that don't have a place, but have faith! Read on to learn how to give these orphans a home.

Picture This!

Lately, I have been using the camera on my phone to help reduce clutter. When I am traveling, I love to create mind maps and make notes about future projects, or designs for marketing campaigns. But when I return to the office, I don't have files for these random thoughts or barely-started book outlines. So, instead of allowing them to litter my desk for who-knows-how-long, I simply take a picture, email it to myself, file it in a clearly labeled file folder on my computer, and recycle the paper original. If it's a bring-forward, I just create a task in Outlook, with the picture attached. It's simple, quick, and totally convenient for when you want to pick up where you left off when the plane landed. In fact, my new web design was created this way.

One client who took our advice cleaned off her desk, created a new filing system for Bring Forward items, and initiated a program to spend time coaching her staff. "I am so proud of myself," she said, when asked about the results. "When I made these simple changes, I began to feel differently about my day. I have more time for what is important, and I don't feel the tension by mid-afternoon that I used to feel. It's like I have a new office and a new outlook on my work."

The Banker's Box Test

When you first purge your office space, you will likely come across a number of items that have questionable value. These could be hand-written notes you took at some brainstorming meetings, information from suppliers, brochures from a conference you attended some months back, or research information on your industry. In an ideal world, you would take time to look at all of these things, sort them, and then file them.

But you haven't got the time, and now they are distractions that clutter your mind with more must-do items.

Here's a neat idea I use from time to time, that saves a lot of grief and gives me instant clutter relief.[35] Start a new banker's box. Label it 'WAS' (Wait-And-See), and mark it with a date exactly one month later. Next, put all those errant, miscellaneous, and questionable papers, reports, notes, and what-have-yous in the box, and store it out of sight.

In your Day-Timer or in Outlook Tasks, pick the one-month-later date and enter, "Check status of WAS box." Then forget about it, and get back to work. In one month, retrieve the box, scan the contents, and toss anything that has no value. My guess is that just about everything will go.

---

35.   This idea is similar to the 'One Month test' on page 134.

The Habit of Completion

As a youth, I can remember watching staff in my father's accounting office working on a client file. Rarely were they interrupted by people or the phone (and they certainly didn't have email); they simply worked on the file in front of them until it was complete, or until they couldn't proceed further because some information was missing. But that was in the twentieth century!

In the new era of distraction, completion of work is harder than ever. And yet it is completion of our plans and goals that is the true measure of success.

When you catch yourself bouncing from your day planner to unfinished emails to paper on your desk—stop! Remind yourself that your goal is to work on the highest priority task at hand, and to complete it before moving on to the next task.

I know I can easily let a well-planned morning run amuck, as I switch from working on a proposal, to responding to a phone call request, to checking how that will work with our shopping cart, which leads to a phone call to our tech person, after which I . . . you get the picture, right?

Your new habit will be to turn off the email (minimizing the screen is a good start), turn away from other distractions, and work diligently on one task until you get it done. And when a new request comes in, you either prioritize it and tackle it later, or use your Two-Minute Rule to do it now.

A large Boulder probably won't get completed in one sitting, but you can definitely complete Pebbles, which gets you going in the right direction. After that, note what needs to be done next and by when, and move on to the next task.

Take Reset Breaks

Just like a reboot for your computer, in order to improve performance, you sometimes need to clear the clutter in your mind.

Continually jumping from one task to another tires the brain, creates stress, and makes decision-making difficult. Latent thoughts and worries have a nagging habit of popping up when you need to be focused on your work at hand. Reset breaks allow you to switch synapse gears to less worrisome thoughts, so that you can return to work with full concentration restored.

It's like taking your car to get serviced. Yes, you have to stop using it for a short while, but when you get it back, it's ready to roll again at full performance.

Just taking a five-minute break to walk, get a drink of water, or stretch, can be enough to reduce the stress load and allow you to refocus on priorities with renewed energy. According to Dr. Brent Coker, a professor in the Department of Management and Marketing at the University of Melbourne, "People need to zone out for a bit to get back their concentration, which in turn leads to a more productive workforce." It's another of the ironic wonders of nature: often you need to do less, in order to do more.

I used to think that the best way to take a break was to grab a bunch of notes and a notepad and head off to the local café to work from a more creative location. While the physical change of environment does improve my concentration, I find I can reproduce this same effect by simply thinking about something different for a few moments.

For example, I might read part of a novel or a magazine article, doodle on a note pad, or just sit quietly and daydream. It amazes me how quickly my mind can feel refreshed and ready to refocus on work with renewed energy. As my wise mother used to say: "A change is as good as a break."

"Hum Me a Tune . . ."

Much research has been done on the effect of music on our brain waves and relaxation. The results, as you would probably expect, are that music can be pretty distracting; enough so that it is actually difficult for you to do your work effectively. If you have a habit of tuning in to a local radio station at work, you can expect that your productivity and ability to concentrate are now competing with the Top 40 hits and invitations to the weekend furniture warehouse sale.

Meanwhile, music can be used to relax you and even stimulate centers of the brain. Daniel Levitin, professor of psychology and behavioral neuroscience at McGill University, recommends having three- to four-minute music reset breaks to stimulate the brain and relax. The choice of music, obviously, is important. Baroque music (think Vivaldi, Bach, Handel, etc.) is widely considered to be the de facto choice, with its sixty beats per minute closely matching our resting heart rate. I find that listening to Baroque late in the evening is soothing without being a mental distraction, and is perfect for concentrating on reading or writing.

Give Your Orphans a Home

Now that you are valuing your workspace, it's likely that you will find that some items don't have a home. They don't belong in your filing system, but you also don't want to see them every day. These could be brochures for upcoming conferences, notes from phone conversations, reports to be completed, or even mail to be read. Go into most any office and you can spot these attention-stealing culprits. Little piles on top of filing cabinets, or small stacks on the carpet or tucked away on the side of the desk. We call these "orphans."

Here's a list of orphans commonly found in office spaces. Just for fun, put a check mark beside the ones decorating your space:

- Sticky notes, with phone numbers or usernames and passwords
- Brochures for conferences you are considering attending
- A Request for Proposal (RFP) you are trying to complete
- Notes from a seminar you attended (two months ago)
- A magazine article someone dropped off for you to read
- Client files that you are working on
- Ideas you scribbled on your last flight
- Receipts from a trip
- Staff schedules
- Bring-forward items that will need your attention in the future
- Notes for a presentation you are working on
- Notes from a meeting you need to review
- Business cards you want to enter into your database
- Unread mail
- Notes from a phone conversation
- A committee file that you need to review

Got a long list of check marks? Great! Now read on for solutions . . .

Action Filing System

I have been using the Action Filing System for about five years, and it has literally transformed my office space.[36] It allows me to handle more projects without feeling as though I'm sinking in worry and details. This simple system also allows me to tie all my miscellaneous pieces of work to my Outlook Tasks. Here's how it works:

Identify all the paperwork that fills your flat spaces (see your list above) and doesn't have an obvious home. Before you move a piece of paper into this new system, consider its value, and make a decision: **Do it, Defer it, Delegate it, or Dump it,** or move it into the Action Filing System.

Create a simple A-Z Action Filing System by dedicating one drawer in your desk for this (or get a portable accordion-style file folder). To organize all of the various orphans, you need to have A-Z tabs.

For each piece of paper, report, DVD, magazine, or 'whatever' that doesn't seem to have a home, follow these steps:

1) Put the item in one of the A-Z hanging folders or slots in the filing unit, under a letter that relates to the topic. For example, for a conference you are thinking of attending, file it under 'C' for conference.

2) Record the action in your Outlook Tasks list (or wherever you record long-term Pebbles) as, "Decide on conference in Vancouver AF-C." The 'AF-C' indicates that this paper is in Action File drawer 'C'.

3) If you are using Microsoft Outlook, remember to select a Category for your task, so that you can have an organized list in Tasks.

---

36. This idea came from *To Do Doing Done!* by G. Lynne Snead and Joyce Wycoff (Fireside, 1997).

4) Enter the date by which the decision needs to be made, or the action taken.

Presto—you're done! Now, enjoy not seeing that distraction every day, knowing that it's recorded, and that you will be reminded only when you need to be.

Once you get into the habit of using this system, you will be amazed at all the annoying pieces of paper, handwritten notes, and brochures that finally have a home. And remember that, not only are you doing yourself a favor by getting all of those trivial thoughts out of your RAM, you are setting a great example for your staff.

Clutter Worksheet

Cleaning up the clutter in your workspace can help you lower your stress level, become more productive, and feel better about your work.

For dealing with paper that comes into my workspace, I am committing to the following one-time system changes (set up an Action Filing System, etc.):

....

....

....

....

....

....

To keep the clutter to a minimum, I am committing to the following new habits (the five-minute purge, etc.):

....

....

....

....

....

....

"Simplicity is the key to brilliance."

—BRUCE LEE, actor and cultural icon

Before You Move On . . .

> *Have you got some unfinished business?*
> *Is there something holding you back?*
> *Are you thinking for your self*
> *Or are you following the pack?*
>
> —BOB DYLAN, "Are you ready?"

How are you doing? Since you have reached this point in the book, you are already among the top five percent of readers who actually get beyond the first half of a business book. Congratulations!

Before I move on to Part III, *Habits* (one of my favorite topics), I want to give you a chance to review what we have already covered, and to look again at what will create real value for you. In most cases, the strategies I am recommending require less than a ten-minute commitment to get started (so there's no excuse).

Plan like a Pilot

This is about working from an Action Plan and a Day Plan, and using goals to stay on track. The big lesson here is to plan ahead and to think one week at a time (your Action Plan). Stay focused on achieving just a few objectives that will move your Boulders ahead each week. Stay away from low-value distractions, and return to your Action Plan after interruptions.

You Come First

Remember: "Those who don't have goals are ruled by those who do." Block time, close your door, coach others, and create resources for them to get answers without you. It's not the individual interruptions today that count—it's the same pattern continuing all year that has the real cost.

Put Meetings on a Diet

Start with a review, then focus on one to three small improvements— or eliminate unnecessary meetings altogether. If you work in a team, have the team design the changes. The more they own the solutions, the better these solutions will be in the long term.

Exorcise your Email

Ten minutes saved a day equals one week of new-found time a year— that should be a good motivator! Check your email less often, set up folders with rules, and learn shortcut keys. Don't allow email to be your default time-filler, and you will be on your way to reclaiming your precious time and attention.

Clearing the Clutter

This is a no-brainer. Take fifteen minutes every Friday afternoon and purge, push, or pull everything off your desk (and floor). Do this for your brain—not just because it's a nice thing to do. Try this for one month, and I guarantee you will feel more creative, relaxed, and taller (at least two of these will happen).

Throughout this book, you have been making notes in the worksheets at the end of each chapter (you have, right?). For each system, look at the action steps you want to make. Are the required steps clear? Is it clear when you are going to take these steps? Who can you ask to support you?

Take a few minutes now to transfer these ideas over to your Boulders list and your Action Plan. Commit your plan to paper (or computer planner tool) now and start to enjoy the benefits of better systems.

And now, it is time to look at your habits . . .

Part III

HABITS

Daily actions to ensure your success

Well, it's 1 am. I'd better go home
and spend some quality time with the kids.

—HOMER SIMPSON, philosopher

Habits of Heroes

*The difference between what we are doing
and what we are capable of doing
would solve most of the world's problems.*

—MAHATMA GANDHI, spiritual leader of India

How did you wake up this morning? Did you turn off the alarm, stand up and stretch, switch on the coffee maker, and fetch the morning paper? Or maybe you went from coffee to email to walking your dog. Some research suggests that as much as 90% of what we do is habit-driven. It makes sense—we couldn't possibly think through everything we do in a day. If we had to do it consciously, the multitude of decisions about where to go, what to eat, what to say, and how to act would immobilize us. Instead, we go with well-worn patterns and routines, to save time and reduce the mental grind.

What about at work? Do you have a routine so well-practiced that you are often on autopilot, going through a pattern that unconsciously unfolds throughout the day?

Of course, some habits serve us well, like taking health breaks (walking, stretching, or refueling with a healthy snack), or taking good notes in a meeting that still make sense a week later. Equally so, some habits don't serve us.

According to The Nielson Company, the average North American watches between fifteen and thirty hours of television each week, whereas research by Thomas J. Stanley, author of the best-selling series, *The Millionaire Next Door*, reveals that the average millionaire watches a mere four hours or less.[37] Do you think there's a connection?

Here's another example: Like many people, your habit is to entertain yourself on your commute to and from work by listening to music in your car, or maybe on your MP3 player, as you take the train, cycle, or walk. But did you know that, at sixty minutes per day (assuming a thirty-minute commute each way), in three years, you will have spent about the same amount of time commuting as a student spends in class earning a college degree?[38] That's a lot of learning opportunity lost to the local DJ's patter, repeats of the morning news (mostly negative), and unwanted updates on celebrity infidelity scandals.

---

37. According to The Nielson Company's 2009 survey, Americans watch more television every year (141 hours a month per person). The number of TVs per household is also increasing, with an average of 2.86 televisions for every 2.5 people (54% of households own three or more sets).

38. The average commute in Canada, where I live, is thirty minutes each way. If you live near a large city, like Vancouver, Toronto, or Montreal, your commute is around sixty minutes each way.

Podcasts and Downloads

I have become a huge fan of downloading podcasts for my commutes, runs, and for walking the dog. I can combine some exercise or travel with a little light learning; it's incredibly easy and, for the most part, free. You can get weekly podcasts, interviews, lectures, and entire books read by the author. I find it is one of the most convenient ways for me to get some new ideas, and have them archived so I can review them later if needed. If you have an iPhone or other device that allows for note-taking, you can also jot a note for later follow-up.[39]

If it's true that we are habitual by nature, then much of our success in life (our happiness, finances, and health), as well as our failures and disappointments, must be a result of habits.

It follows, then, that there is a simple cause-effect relationship available: change a habit; change your results.

At work, you may have habits that continually trip you up, such as answering that last phone call instead of getting to the meeting on time, or constantly checking your email, even though you have important work to complete.

In this chapter, we will look at habits that can immediately help you excel at making time work for you.

I practice and teach the following eight habits—and they work. In fact, the results can be impressive. By adopting a new habit, seminar participants have been able to free up enormous amounts of time each week, take better care of their health, and arrive at work with the kind of energy and attitude that makes every day great.

---

39. I've included some of my favorite podcasts at www.hughculver.com/breakbook.

Your job is to find the habits that work for you, and to practice them for at least thirty days.

Here's a quick overview of what I will be covering:

1) **Jump-Start Your Day** – Get new strategies to guarantee a great day—every day.

2) **Honor the Mundane** – Discover the hidden blessing in even the most routine task.

3) **Go with the Flow** – Learn how to match your task to your energy and make work easier.

4) **Make it the Day Before Vacation** – Employ daily strategies to adopt a 'must do' attitude.

5) **Put Procrastination on Pause** – Once and for all, learn to overcome avoidance.

6) **Make Time for Me-Time** – Practice actively refueling, recharging, and restoring your energy.

7) **Start a Stop-Doing List** – Clear the space for what is most important by removing what isn't.

8) **Celebrate Successes** – Be your own cheerleader and teach your brain to anticipate a pay-off.

1

• • •

Jump-Start Your Day

*I'm good enough, I'm smart enough
and doggone it, people like me!*
—STUART SMALLEY, Saturday Night Live

Can you imagine a high-performing athlete showing up for a competition, thinking, ""I think I'll just see how it goes and hope for the best." It would be ludicrous—and more than likely disasterous!

We all know that athletes need to properly prepare for a competition. They make sure they get enough sleep, eat well, check their equipment, and repeatedly envision a successful competition. In fact, most coaches would argue that an athlete's attention to preparation could easily make or break their competition.

So why should preparation for work be any different?

We spend about one-third of our working years at work. Don't you think that is too much time to leave to chance?

Every day, either consciously or unconsciously, we choose how we come to work. We might think that the quality of our day is determined by outside circumstances: how people drive on their morning commutes, the line-up at Starbucks, or how heavy our workload is. In fact, what determines the quality of our day, more than anything else, are *intentions* and *choices*.

When you jump-start your day, you consciously pre-empt the day with a clear picture of the success you look forward to creating. You choose to see the big picture, instead of short-term frustrations. You choose to stay focused on your goals and to continually make the decisions that allow you to complete tasks. You plan to create the best possible success for yourself and for others, despite whatever crisis others find themselves in. In short, you don't leave your day to chance. In the words of Abraham Lincoln, ". . . your own resolution to succeed is more important than any other one thing."

True Confessions

For many years, my morning routine between waking and leaving for work was admittedly a disaster. Every morning, I wanted to pack in as much work, exercise, and time with my family as I could, but

it wasn't working. My unrealistic expectations left me frustrated, and my family resigned to my chaotic rushing.

About eight years ago, I decided to take a close look at what wasn't working, and I found someone to blame (guess who?). I realized that, while I aspired to enjoy productive mornings, where I was free to focus on my activity of choice, I was delusional in my planning. Instead of enjoying both my time *and* family time, I wasn't enjoying either. I was typically absent from breakfast and was instead either frantically trying to finish some work, or halfway through a workout.

It was a recipe for disaster, and I was the chef.

"For those of you headed to the office, today's forecast calls for scattered frustration, followed by a brief storm of criticism and a flurry of random distractions."

My first change was to go to bed earlier (I am usually comatose after about 10 pm, so this was an easy commitment to make). Then I experimented with my routine, and settled on rising at 5 am, staying off the email, and being more realistic about my goals.[40] I also became almost fanatical about planning the first two hours of the morning the night before.

This last change was no big deal—all it took was a couple of

---

40. Okay, I'm aware that getting up at 5 am isn't for everyone—this just happens to work for me. The important point is that one new habit has led to years of positive benefits.

minutes to scratch out a quick note of my plan for the morning. On a typical morning, it might read:

- Finish proposal

- Blog

- 6:15 paddle

- 7:15 walk Riley (dog)

- Kate (daughter) needs ride to school

But the payoff has been huge. I now have almost two hours every morning to read, write, work on Boulders, and exercise. My morning time has become sacred space, and is incredibly important to my sense of achievement and peace. It is the one time of the day when I can think, write, and exercise, guaranteed that I will not be interrupted.

Let's look at four other strategies for jump-starting *your* day:

Envision Success

Just like athletes, we can create more success by envisioning the best possible outcomes for ourselves. If you have a heavy workload or tough meeting planned for the day, spend a minute to see it going well. Your prediction for success will lift your mood and help create a positive attitude.

This isn't 1990s positive thinking; your brain is actually hardwired to spot more of what you want. Let me explain.

Prehistorically, we were constantly on the lookout for our survival needs: food, a mate, safety, and shelter (of course, not always in that order). Through natural selection, we evolved to have a kind of built-in radar for what we want, be it that certain model of Toyota, the new iPhone, or a sunny vacation destination.

Even though we're not running around the Savanna half-naked, fighting for survival, our highly attuned internal radar is busy at work. Once you create the focus on what you want, you will become more aware of examples of it around you.

You could be zooming along the highway, thinking about work, when you suddenly spot the model of car you like. Out of hundreds of cars, and in only a split second, you managed to pick out the one car four lanes away. You even noticed the tinted windows or paint color that you like. That's a pretty powerful focus.

This classic, self-fulfilling prophecy (I tend to get more of what I am looking for) can be put to work for positive results as well.

Moments before I step on stage to give a speech, I create a powerful mental focus on how *I want to* feel in front of the audience. I know I want to feel calm, but excited, resourceful, and ready to share. I create the image in my mind, and allow my body to respond emotionally.

Within seconds of stepping on stage, I start to notice examples of feeling pretty good, and of even having fun. I see someone in the audience having a good time listening to my crazy story about flying to the South Pole. I notice my body feels relaxed and loose. I realize that I've just delivered one of my lessons, and wasn't using my notes (which I always take as a sign of being comfortable).

As I notice these clues, I remind myself that everything is working: I'm relaxed, the audience is engaged, the timing is good—it's working. I think to myself: 'I *can* be giving a speech *and* having a heck of a good time!' Perfect! Now I'm in the state I need to be in to perform at my best. No longer am I fixated on A/V set-up and timing details; I'm in the moment, doing my thing, and getting rewarded for it.

Envisioning success is also a great exercise for your morning commute. Take just a moment to envision the sales meeting going well, and getting the 'Yes' you are looking for. See the list in your Day Plan becoming smaller as you cross off Pebbles. Envision yourself enjoying an afternoon walk and feeling successful and happy with your accomplishments.

It only takes a few minutes, but the impact can last all day, and can make the difference between having just another day at work, or feeling powerful, successful, and in control.

Prepare for the Games

> *Only after you take care of yourself*
> *can you take care of other business.*
> —ELLEN DEGENERES, comedian, TV show host

Are you taking care of the basics? Do you get enough sleep, exercise regularly, and eat a good breakfast? All the mental machinations in the world can't overcome the drag of an engine that's running on empty. It's pretty simple: if you neglect your body, you will pay the price in terms of concentration, energy, emotions, and health. The trick is to establish a routine that will fuel your engine. My rule is that if it's convenient, affordable, and enjoyable, I'll probably stick with it. Here are some of the basics.[41]

Stay hydrated. Coffee and tea don't hydrate you; in fact they are diuretics that draw water out of your cells. You may have noticed that drinking more tea can actually leave you with a dry mouth. Pounding back the mugs of java, or sipping your favorite leaf brew, makes for sluggish circulation—your heart has to work harder, and your body starts to redirect blood away from areas not vital for survival (like the brain). A simple solution is to start the day with a large glass of water. That will get you off to a great start. Then, you need to match every cup of coffee or tea with a glass of water.

---

41. Obviously, you need to always seek professional medical advice before attempting any significant change in diet or fitness.

Exercise at least thirty minutes per day. Okay, let's get real about exercise. It may not be a scientifically accurate research study, but every time I ask an audience if they would like to be in better physical shape, virtually all hands go up. This leads to the first fact: almost everyone wants to be in better physical shape. Second fact: most people are never going to commit to a regular exercise routine. Third fact: people will commit to something they enjoy. No wonder TV wins over exercise, along with reading, eating, surfing the Internet, and a host of other distractions.

So the desire is there, but not the will. The mismatch is that 'exercise' sounds like work, not something to be enjoyed. The solution should be obvious: *make exercise something you enjoy.*

First, commit to a goal, whether it's to look better in the mirror, enter that running race, complete the cycling tour, or just feel better in the morning. Next, start a routine that you actually look forward to. Combine your walk or time on the stationary bike with listening to an audio book or podcast. Join a riding club, sports team, or hiking group. Or stretch yourself (literally) with yoga, Tai Chi, or Karate.

Once you have your goal and preferred way to get there, stick with it, despite real or imagined distractions. It's like an Olympic athlete once said, "There's only two times you need to exercise to be prepared for the Olympics: when you want to and when you don't."

Walk a Dog—It's Good for You

After over twenty years of pretty consistent training for marathons, Riley made me cut back on my workouts. Riley is our new dog, and dogs (as I quickly learned) need a lot of exercise. So my runs and long bike rides have turned into morning and night walks—every day. And here's the surprise: sixty to ninety minutes of brisk walking a day (we run together on weekends) is a lot of exercise. Even though these weren't the intensive workouts I was used to, this was more consistent, and involved a lot of hours with a leash. So I did some research:

It turns out that thirty minutes of brisk walking, just five days a week, is a fantastic fitness program! In a longitudinal study of 72,000 female nurses, this amount of exercise was associated with a 30 to 40% lower risk of heart disease, reduced risk of breast cancer, and 50% reduced risk of type 2 diabetes.[42] A similar study related this level of exercise to a 20 to 30% lower risk of gallstone surgery in women, and half the risk of strokes in men.[43,44] And the list goes on for general health benefits, like lower risk of hip fracture, arthritis, colon cancer, mood swings, impotence, depression, and osteoporosis.[45]

Not bad results for the same amount of time as watching the evening news!

Eat for long energy. In the morning, skip the pop tarts and go for complex carbohydrates (potatoes, whole grain bread, or cereal) with protein (yogurt, cottage cheese, or skim milk) and fruit. Your

---

42. Based on the twenty year Nurses' Health Study of 72,000 female nurses.
43. A Harvard study of more than 60,000 women ages 40 to 65.
44. According to a Harvard study of more than 11,000 men.
45. Be sure to check with your doctor on the level of exercise that's best for you.

objective is to fuel up for the next four to five hours, so think long-term. The quick hit of pastry or muffin with coffee might work short-term, but you'll be suffering through an energy slump later. Stay away from the high-sugar-content sweets, cereals, or pastries. There is a reason why 'sugar' is first on the list of ingredients for most of these goodies, and it's not because it is good for your health.

Sleep to recharge. The jury is out on how long, but the verdict is that, too little sleep is obviously not good, but nor is too much. If you aren't getting the sleep you need, you need to get it right—this is a catalyst for all aspects of your health. There are many avenues to help, including sleep clinics, books, online resources, and audio programs.

Pack a snack. My wife once defined the muffin, the ubiquitous commuters' treat, as the equivalent of cake, wrapped in paper. Yuck—that re-frame has stuck with me for years, and has kept my paws off many a treat. Let's face it: most snacks and drinks we consume during the day aren't designed for our long-term health. Healthier alternatives, like fruit, nuts, and raw vegetables have to be made more convenient than the vending machine. Every day (even when traveling), bring an interesting variety of healthy goodies and experiment; find out what makes you feel best, and at what time of day.

Avoid the Rush

Do you find yourself rushing to get to meetings on time, rushing to finish that phone call before your next appointment, and then—topping it all off—rushing to get home on time? Constant rushing can cost you, in terms of mistakes made, appointments missed, and elevated stress. It also sets a poor example for anyone who's watching. This constant hurrying is simply a habit, and can be changed.

Here are four solutions that will help you slow your jets and still get it all done. Don't believe me? Read on.

- **Don't start rushed.** Allow enough time to get to work early, so you can get settled in and review your plans for the week and for the day. Pilots don't jump in the seat just before takeoff, and neither should you.

- **Start the day prepared.** At the end of every day, prepare your plan for the next day, and update your Action Plan. Invest just ten minutes in this ritual and enjoy less worry on the drive home, more productivity in the morning, and more decisiveness throughout the day.

- **Allow enough time.** You know that—by the time you prepare for it, attend it, and return to your desk—a 'thirty-minute meeting' actually takes forty-five minutes. So block the actual time needed. Underestimating time needed for meetings, appointments, and Pebbles just sets you up for more rushing—and more stress.

- **Plan to get back on track.** I find that, in the late morning and mid-afternoon, I need a five-minute break to revisit my plan and refocus. It's not a big investment of time, but can make a world of difference to what happens next.

Keep the Focus

By now, you should know I'm a big advocate for minimizing distractions and starting at full speed. If you are like most people, the first ninety minutes of the day are your most productive time, so it's critical that you protect that time.[46] Stay off the email, focus on your Day Plan, and limit interruptions. This is the time to move

---

46. I cover this idea more in the chapter, "Go with the Flow."

Boulders forward, have difficult conversations, make decisions, and cross Pebbles off your list.

Now that you are excited about Jump-Starting Your Day, let's take a closer look at some of the inevitable work—the somewhat dull duties that often cross our path, but that must get done.

2

• • •

Honor the Mundane

If a man is called to be a street sweeper, he should sweep streets even as Michelangelo painted, or Beethoven composed music, or Shakespeare wrote poetry. He should sweep streets so well that all the hosts of heaven and earth will pause to say, 'Here lived a great street sweeper who did his job well.'

—MARTIN LUTHER KING JR., civil rights activist

It happens every day: the mundane, boring, humdrum, and ordinary tasks that don't belong in the life of a successful person like you. Shouldn't your rise to success mean you never have to pay another bill or take out the garbage? Think again—you're human, and we all have to put in our time doing the mundane. In fact, I think it's an essential part of keeping life real, and should be celebrated.

Don't get me wrong. I'm not advocating hanging onto tasks that someone else—or some nifty software—can do, just so you can cross them off your list. But there will always be tasks that can't be outsourced, automated, or dumped, and that someone (like you) has to do. Try looking at those tasks as more than an unwanted irritation.

Instead, they could provide an opportunity to be mindful of, and even grateful for, doing something simple and easy for a change.

As Stephan Rechtschaffen warns in *Timeshifting*, "If we push away the mundane, we push away the present. And when pushing away becomes our habitual pattern, we're likely to push away the extraordinary moments too—unable to fully savor them in our rush to 'get on'."

What is on your list of the 'mundane'?

Opening the mail. With the wide-scale adoption of electronic billing and email, it's become a bit of a novelty to read mail that comes with a stamp. Once a week, I go through the mail: total time—about fifteen minutes. The mechanics of the exercise (slice open the envelope, read, assess, toss, respond, pay the bill, or file) requires little effort, but it can actually be a welcome change of pace to complete such a simple task. Sometimes, I even get ideas for marketing or for improvements to our own correspondence.[47]

Updating records of progress. We use a number of tools to track our progress in sales, type of sales, website analytics, etc. To keep current, each tool requires a few minutes of attention each week. It's not work I relish, but I find the ritual of entering the data and paying attention to empirical results (as opposed to my overly optimistic assessments) very rewarding.

Writing 'thank you' cards. I know, I know—they love you, and you know it. Right. Thanking people for their business, or their help with your business, is another task that competes with other priorities, but also could be one of the best five-minute investments that you make.

---

47. See Habit #7 "Start a Stop-Doing List" for how I changed the way I deal with bill payments.

I remember author and retired CEO, James Autry, saying that one of the best investments he ever made, as the leader of a national printing house, was to start every morning by writing a 'thank you' card to a staff person. As he explained, it always seemed like nothing at the time, but invariably, Autry would visit one of his plants much later, and a worker would approach him to thank him for the card that he still kept. It's mundane, it's routine, but it's a great use of time. Hint: To avoid excuses, keep a stock of 'thank you' cards handy.

Planning a trip. How often have you put off booking flights and hotels for a conference or sales trip, only to find that prices had gone up since you first checked, and your favorite hotel is now full? I'm sure Brad Pitt doesn't book his own flights, but you probably do, and the sooner you act, the sooner you get the satisfaction that comes with completion.

The steps are basic: a little research online, one or two clicks of the mouse, and the deed is done. No late registration charge on the conference, a good rate on the flight, and you got the hotel's best rate. Don't think of it as a 'hassle'; instead, think of it as a simple twenty-minute investment that will save you money.

When I'm on the road, there are many traveling rituals I have to endure: packing and getting to the airport on time, waiting for flights, taxi rides, and check-in at hotels, as well as all the steps needed to prepare for a presentation. It's part of the package that comes with the privilege of being able to speak to audiences.

One of these mundane rituals has, surprisingly, become a favorite meditative moment. When I am on an airplane all day traveling, my workday is usually reserved to the evening hours before the event the next morning. I usually spend two or three hours in final preparation and catching up on other work. The last ritual I have before packing it in for the day is to iron my clothes in preparation for the next day.

Instead of dreading my visit with the ironing board, I actually look at it as a kind of meditation. After all, this is one of the simplest things I will have done all day, so it may be as close to being meditative as I will get.

For about fifteen minutes, I carefully prepare my clothes. I pay close attention to details and intentionally try to think about nothing else. I notice I am very relaxed and unhurried. As I complete the task, I quietly acknowledge my efforts during the day, and give thanks for all the gifts that I have received.

The Buddhist monk, peace activist, and author, Thich Nhat Hanh, describes the value of being fully present in the moment this way: "If I am incapable of washing dishes joyfully, if I want to finish them quickly so I can go and have dessert, I will be equally incapable of enjoying my dessert. With the fork in my hand, I will be thinking about what to do next, and the texture and flavor of the dessert, together with the pleasure of eating it, will be lost. I will always be dragged into the future, never able to live in the present moment."

Take a moment now and consider a task that you often procrastinate about, or do begrudgingly. How could you re-frame it as something more valuable—even as a gift to be honored?

Whether the work is mundane and routine or new and engaging, let's look at how to complete it with less effort by going with the flow.

3

• • •

Go with the Flow

Knowing when not to work hard
is as important as knowing when to.

−HARVEY MACKAY, businessman and author

I t is 2:30 in the afternoon and I feel like my brain has gone on holiday. I just caught myself re-reading a paragraph for the third time (and it still doesn't make any sense). I have two other projects on hold in front of me, and I'm not getting traction on any of them. I don't know if I should keep ploughing ahead, hoping my synapses have enjoyed their midday nap, or try a brew of caffeine. Neither choice seems likely to succeed; I'm in the afternoon doldrums, with no wind in sight.

I think a common fallacy is that—as though we are electrical motors—we should be able to focus and produce the same results throughout the day—just plug us in, and we produce. Minute after minute, hour after hour, we should be focused, concentrating on completion, and pleasant to everyone who crosses our path. Yeah, right.

Of course we know this doesn't happen. We have energy highs, lows, and in-betweens. Our bodies respond to what we eat, when we ate, and how long it's been since we've seen our pillows. There is also the natural fatigue that comes from working hard at thinking for six, seven, or eight hours.

Personal Energy Chart

A better approach is what I call: Go with the Flow. First, ask yourself—when are you the most energetic, optimistic, and ready to tackle the tough stuff on your list? And when do you catch yourself semi-comatose, reading the same paragraph for the third time?

Maybe you notice that often, around 1:30 or 2 pm you are searching for a chocolate bar, pouring another coffee, or snacking on something you will regret later. It feels like your brain has stopped firing and your reaction is to try to give it life support.

And just as it's natural to need sleep, it's also natural for your body to cycle through energy highs and lows. But, rather than trying to jump-start your synapses during an energy slump, a better solution is to *work with* your energy patterns and not fight what is natural. First, let's see what your energy pattern at work really is.

In the chart below, imagine that the horizontal line represents your time at work. The left-hand star represents when you arrive at work, midday is represented by the small triangle, and the end of the day, when you go home, is indicated by the right-hand star. The vertical column represents your energy at any given moment. The higher up the chart, the more energy you have, and the easier it is to get work done while being optimistic, productive, and creative. Conversely, the lower you are on the chart, the less energy you have, and the more difficult it is to concentrate on work or complete tasks.

Now think about your energy during the day.

- When are you the most energetic, focused, optimistic, and resilient?

- When does your energy wane, and you start searching for a sugar snack?

On the first chart, draw a curve, from left to right, to represent your typical energy flow in a day. Again, the higher the line, the more energy you normally have at that time of day, and the lower the line, the lower your energy level.

Draw that line now . . .

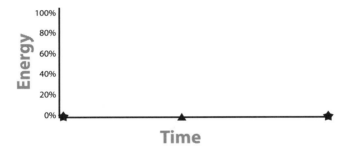

On the second chart, I am showing an average energy curve, with two high-energy periods in the day, based on a study of over 2,200 Canadian workers (conducted by Accutemps).

Don't fret if your chart doesn't match; this is just an example.

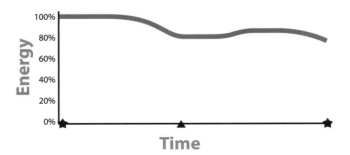

What is important is to distinguish between the 'highs' and 'lows' in the day. If you are like most people, one peak time is in the morning, usually for about ninety minutes, and one is shortly after lunch, which usually lasts about one hour. Again, it doesn't matter if this is true for you—I want you to just focus on where you have 'highs' and 'lows'.

During our high-energy times, our thinking is clear, we have positive energy, and we are more creative. Work is easier, we are happier doing it, and we are far more likely to be efficient and successful at completing it.

But how are *you* using your high-energy zones? And what are you doing in your low-energy zones? If you are like most people, you choose what to work on, based on what is most urgent that day (other than scheduled events, like meetings, of course).

One common pattern I see, in almost every group I work with, is that people start their day with email (low energy work) during what is most people's high energy zone, and try to attack Boulders (high energy work) in low energy zones. It's completely backwards and counterproductive. It's also easily fixed.

On the following chart, I am presenting what an 'ideal' day could look like. I'm suggesting this formula because, in fact, this is what I strive for when I have a day in the office.

Here is a breakdown of my plan for the day:

- First up is a review of my plans. I update what I recorded the night before, or on Friday before I left for the weekend. Having quiet, focused time for fifteen minutes as soon as I arrive guarantees a less stressful, more successful day.

- You might recall that, in the chapter "Exorcise Your Email," I suggested having about four email visits a day. Here is that list again:

- **8:45 am** – After checking my Day and Action Plans, I check email, but only to respond to emergencies, clients, or client-related work that I know was left over from the day before. I delete, click and drag email to Tasks or Calendar, or move email to a folder. Total time: about fifteen minutes.

- **10:30 am** – Check email (about thirty minutes).

- **1:45 pm** – Check email (about fifteen minutes). This is a quick check for returned messages and any important new messages.

- **3:30 pm** – Check email (about thirty minutes). I spend more time composing longer responses and cleaning up the Inbox.

  The total time spent on emails is about one hour to one and one-half hours.

- I have two crucial periods dedicated to Boulder work: before 10:30 am and before 3:30 pm. Each session lasts about forty-five minutes to one hour long.

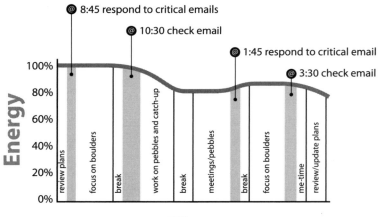

- There are a couple of undedicated flex-time slots built into the day, for scheduling conference calls or catching up on client work.

- The end of the day is important Me-Time, for setting the stage for the following day. I like to have thirty minutes to do some reading, wrap up some Boulder work, or make appointments.

- I finish with my planning ritual: check my Action Plan, update my Day Plan, and acknowledge what I have accomplished. The more I focus on what is going well with my work and my progress toward my goals, the more excited I am about returning to it the next day.

Consider the routines you have now. Are you making the best use of your high-energy zones and your low-energy zones? Chances are that your energy patterns are predictable, so it just makes sense to work *with them*, instead of against.

Is Your Work Really Unpredictable?

Simon oversees procurement in a food processing company that makes fruit juices and snack bars. He often finds himself responding to immediate needs from suppliers and staff, as well as negotiating long-term contracts for the supply of fruit. When I showed him the 'Go with the Flow' model, he was skeptical. The unpredictable nature of his job had convinced Simon that he needed to be in reaction mode all day. At the same time, he complained that he frequently found himself struggling to do financial planning when his energy was low.

We all have repetitive work (reading email, returning phone calls, making sales calls, and filling in forms or schedules), and we have some unpredictable work (receiving phone calls, managing interruptions, and attending impromptu meetings). Once you identify the nature of the various tasks, you can start to schedule them at your high-energy times (if they require your full concentration) or low-energy times (if the work is routine and less taxing).

Simon now organizes his day around his high-energy and low-energy time slots. For example, he makes calls to suppliers before 10:30 am, when his energy is up and he knows they will be in their offices. He does the bulk of his email work after 10:30 am and between 2 and 3 pm, when his energy is low, and he leaves most of the afternoon for emergencies and paperwork.

"It's not a perfect system," Simon reported after one month of working with his new schedule. "Stuff still comes up, but I feel like I have a game plan and, even when my energy is low, I am still being productive."

Harness Your High-Energy Zones

Here are some strategies that can help you harness your high-energy zones and get more work done in less time:

- **Protect your high-energy zones.** If you are a morning person, minimize your time on email for the first ninety minutes, close your door, and let people in your office know that mornings are when you need uninterrupted time to work on your Boulders. If you plan for it, you can accomplish 80% of your work in this time zone.

- **Reschedule meetings.** Move meetings to outside your high-energy periods. Unless they are brainstorming or problem-solving meetings, you will do everyone a favor if you hold routine meetings just before or after lunch. If it is a creative-thinking meeting, try to schedule it before 11 am.

- **Cluster similar tasks together.** When you tackle similar tasks together (whether they be: sales calls, creative writing, or email), you minimize lost time between tasks and benefit from momentum. As an example, I often notice that when I make all my sales calls in one bundle of time the energy from one call feeds the next and each subsequent call becomes easier to make.

- **Make a plan.** Always make a Day Plan for the next day before leaving the office. Make sure you know what you will work on first thing in the morning, and block that time on your calendar.

- **Complete tasks.** Before moving on to other tasks, finish the task you are working on. Avoid multi-tasking (especially in low-energy periods), focus on completion, and work on getting the Pebbles off your Day Plan.

- **Be realistic.** Get into a habit of setting realistic targets for each time slot. Only thirty minutes? Plan for twenty-five minutes of work, and actually complete it before moving on.

The following Pebbles are great candidates to include in your high-energy zones:

- Doing creative planning with your team or committee

- Checking on a committee's progress since the last meeting

- Making critical phone calls that require your full attention

- Resolving a relationship issue

- Writing 'thank you' cards

- Making sales calls of any kind, or follow-up calls to clients

- Performing feedback, coaching, and staff performance reviews

- Interviewing job applicants

– Composing a critical communication by letter or email

– Planning an event

– Making critical budget or staffing decisions

Here's a good rule-of-thumb if you tend to procrastinate about certain tasks: it probably needs to be rescheduled to a high-energy time. This is where I put my writing assignments, proposal writing, and calls with clients. It feels great to cross the tough tasks off my list and cruise into some flex time, knowing that the hard push is behind me.

Now it's time to learn how to go on vacation . . . for free!

4

• • •

Make it the Day
Before Vacation

*Vacation is what you take when you can't take
what you've been taking any longer.*

–COWARDLY LION, *The Wizard of Oz*

"That's a nice tan," I commented to the woman seated to my left at a project committee meeting. "Have you been on vacation?"

After she shared details of a tranquil sojourn on some sunny Mexican beach, I asked her the question I was *really* curious about: "What was work like, the day *before* you left for vacation?"

"It was crazy," she exclaimed with a mischievous grin. "I was so determined to complete everything on my list that nothing got in my way. Even my desk was clear for the first time in months!"

Amazing! She had created a new experience at work, and she hadn't gone anywhere yet.

Has this ever happened to you?

I call this the "Day Before Vacation" phenomenon. It's the experience of being totally focused on completion, incredibly resilient to distractions, optimistic, and energetic—yet nothing has physically changed. It's still you at the same job, with the same work demands, but having a completely different experience. You are focused on an exciting goal, and you won't let anything get in your way.

> It's not what we don't know that prevents us from succeeding; it's what we know that just ain't so that is our greatest obstacle.
> —JOSH BILLINGS, author

Another client described this experience as, "One of the most productive days of my year. My desk was clear, loose papers were gone, and my list was complete—it simply had to be!"

The reality is that we can create whatever experience we want, whenever we want. We could certainly do this as children. Watch children at play, and see how quickly they can change their moods, from happy to sad to concerned to curious, and back to happy. As adults, we are simply out of practice.

In his book, *Mozart's Brain and the Fighter Pilot*, Richard Restak explains the value of choosing positive thoughts. "Since the brain can only feature in the foreground one thought at a time, our choice of a positive thought and our concentration on it robs the painful thought of its sting."

Remember, whatever experience you create in your mind, you will naturally look for evidence to prove it's true. If you think you have too much work to do, guess what you'll notice? And if you worry that you can't seem to complete any work with all the distractions in your day, then guess what you are going to get more of?

What if, for a change, you decide to *feel* productive, effective, and decisive? You hold an image of yourself cheerfully completing work and crossing it off your list. Now guess what evidence you will start to notice?

The key principle is that you can create whatever experience you want at work. You just need to make the choice, change what you focus on, and then notice evidence that supports your way of thinking. Remember, once we make up our mind about what we want, we look for evidence to prove we are right, and we become the author of our own self-fulfilling prophecy.

To get that Day Before Vacation experience anytime you want, try these simple ideas:

- **Envision what you want.** On your way to work, take two minutes to envision what you want the day to look like. Use adjectives like successful, energized, and skillful. Remember, the conscious brain can only focus on one thought at a time, so give it a powerful, convincing picture.

- **Make your goals visible.** Organize your workspace so that your Day Plan and Action Plan are always visible. These two lists are your anchor to what is most important. Every afternoon, update your Day Plan from your Action Plan. Review the lists often, look forward to crossing items off, and revise your priorities as necessary.

- **Avoid distractions.** Start your day determined to complete the tasks on your Day Plan first. Focus on one task at a time, complete each one before moving on, and notice your success building.

- **Do the hardest work first.** Sales calls, proposal writing, staff performance issues, and tough decisions should all be tackled first thing in the day. Getting buried in emails is just avoidance of the inevitable. Do yourself a favor and start the day ready to tackle the hardest work first.

- **Break work into small chunks.** When you break Pebbles into smaller chunks, the steps you need to take become obvious. You can more easily complete them, cross them off your Day Plan, and get the positive feeling of completion. For example, if you need to plan a meeting, you could break that down into:

  - Secure meeting room

  - Send out meeting invitations

  - Review the last agenda and create new draft agenda

  - Circulate agenda for feedback

  - Order food, catering, A/V, etc.

- **Return to your goals.** A great trick—after any interruption—is to always return to your Action Plan, and then to your Day Plan. The objective is to keep your focus on the long-term, while tracking your progress on the current work.

The Joy of Completion

I love crossing Pebbles off my Day Plan. The more items crossed off, the better I feel, and the more I want to keep going. Sometimes I even break single Pebbles into smaller pieces, just so I have more to cross off my list. For example, 'Follow up on sales lead' can be broken down into: 'call enquiry back', 'diarize follow-up call', and 'send a thank-you note'.

Sometimes, I'll even put routine Pebbles on my list just to cross them off, like: 'pack for seminar', 'update A/R', and 'draft blog'.

Exercise Your BOAs

In thirty years of triathlons, road races, and marathons, I've never been passed by a bunny, especially not one sporting the markings '3:15' in thick black lines on its ears. This bunny was a very fit-looking runner leading ten more runners, and its ears were a bright pink, fuzzy pair strapped to his hat.

To add insult to injury, not only did these runners quite handily pass me about ninety minutes into my marathon race, they also appeared to be comfortably chatting with each other and having a good time!

A few seconds after passing me, they suddenly slowed to a brisk walking pace.

Immediately I could feel the urge to seek revenge and I quickened my pace. But something wasn't right. The walking looked planned, not the result of the exhaustion that you would typically see this far into a marathon.

At the time, I had no idea that many runners now train to run as a pack, following a 'bunny' (the numbers on his ears were the group's planned finish-time). Their strategy is to run for ten minutes and walk for one. Rather than being slower, this strategy has proven to extend athletic endurance, and to produce faster finish times. By the way, after about twenty minutes, the pack (still happily chatting away) was so far ahead of me, they were out of sight!

Just like the runners, research has found that we are most effective when we focus for what I call "Bursts of Attention" (BOA). Just like a Boa constrictor that squeezes its prey and then relaxes, a BOA is an intense period of focus followed by a short break.

If you are going to tackle a big project, work with your full attention for about twenty minutes, then stand and take a break. The trick is to relax just as fully as you focus. I find that a short bit of activity helps me unwind and get centered again. Something as simple as standing up and walking across the office to refill my water glass shifts my energy and allows me to refocus.

Avoid the temptation to go back to email, or to get distracted by the paper on your desk. A break is a break. Savor the few minutes of respite, distract your thinking with light reading or a walk, and then mentally plan to re-engage.

Balance between short BOAs and energy breaks, and you will be amazed at what you can accomplish, and at how focused you will become.

Refocus on the Big Picture

The first rule in a skid, when your car loses traction and starts to slide, is to look where you want to go. However, anyone who has lost control of a car on an icy or wet road knows full well that your instinct is to become fixated on what you *want to avoid*. Strangely, this instinct won't serve you very well.

Rather than helping you to maneuver around the obstacle, staring at what you want to avoid actually tends to draw you closer. This explains why, more often than you might expect, the lone driver on some remote country road manages to crash into the only telephone pole in sight.

Try this while driving your car (when you have full control over it). After taking your eyes off the road for a few seconds, try returning your focus to the road *immediately in front* of your car. You will quickly realize that, unless you are crawling along in a school zone, you can't navigate this way. When we drive, we need to focus on where *we need to go,* and far enough in the future to make all the necessary small adjustments to get there. In fact, the faster you drive, the further down the road you should focus.

Similarly, at work, the solution in a 'skid' (when you are overwhelmed with distractions) is to refocus on the big picture, not on the minutiae that fills your day. The busier you are, the more you should be looking at your Action Plan and at what needs to get completed this week.

When you look at the big picture in your Action Plan, you shift your attention away from low-value distractions and toward your priorities. So it makes sense that the Action Plan should be the anchor in your day, and that you should constantly refocus on it.

Periodically stop what you are doing and review your progress. What is going well? What have you accomplished? Are your time estimates for the remaining tasks realistic? What do you need to change in your priorities?

Harvey Mackay, author of *Swim with the Sharks Without Being Eaten Alive*, had a habit of reassessing his plan throughout the day, looking at what could still be completed, what needed to be moved, and what could be delegated or dropped. His big picture view and triage approach to planning will always be more successful than staying fixated solely on the immediate issue you are on a collision course with.

Act Like an Optimist

Your mind has a curious habit of following your body's lead. If you are dragging yourself around the office, feeling low-energy and acting like you need a nap, your mind will pick up on these clues and start to focus on how tired you are. It's a self-fulfilling prophecy, kicked off by how you carry your body. The more you act tired ('Gee, I'm feeling tired'), the more you will feel tired.

> *Habits of thinking need not be forever. One of the most significant findings in psychology in the last twenty years is that individuals can choose the way they think.*
>
> —MARTIN SELIGMAN, author and director of the Positive Psychology Center

Often in my seminars, I give participants the experience of a mind-body disconnect. First, I ask the group to take on a physiological position of being tired, despondent, or of hopelessness. Some people will slump over in their chairs and put their heads in their hands, others will put their heads on the table. Just watching their exaggerated performances usually makes *me* feel sleepy!

Next, I instruct the group to freeze in this physical position and, once I see that they are completely sunk into their self-imposed stupor, I ask them to immediately switch to feeling intense happiness and joy, but without moving. After some initial shock, I start to hear a growing wave of snickering and laughter. While their brains are sending instructions to their bodies to feel good, there isn't a lot of cooperation coming from the body.

It's like the Charlie Brown cartoon, where Charlie, slumped over and looking thoroughly dejected, says to Lucy, "This is my depressed stance." Charlie goes on to explain. "It makes a lot of difference how you stand. The worst thing you can do is to stand up straight and hold your head high. Because then you'll start to feel better. If you are going to get any joy out of being depressed, you have to stand like this."

One of the simplest ways to adopt the Day Before Vacation attitude is to sit up in your chair, hold your head high, push your shoulders back, look up, smile, and act like an optimist. When you walk into a meeting, or go to get a glass of water, walk with determination and focus. The more you act like a successful person, the more your mind will tune into clues that prove you are right. In fact, psychologists claim that the phenomenon of 'state-dependent memory' will bring to mind thoughts and memories from when you experienced the same emotion in the past.[48]

To describe this strategy a bit more succinctly: Fake it until you make it!

---

48.   http://www.trans4mind.com/life-coach/life-challenge10/kraus.shtml

Notice how some people seem to go through the motions of moving their body without much attention. It's a zombie-like psychosis, adopted over years, and left unchecked. Now notice successful people around you, and watch how they carry themselves. Someone moving with determination and a spirit of confidence is unconsciously programming his or her mind for success.

Paying attention to how you carry *your body* and intentionally feeling optimistic can launch you into that Day before Vacation anytime. It may not compare to a week in Cancun, but it's available all day every day, and you don't ever have to worry about losing your luggage.

Now that our bags are packed, let's look at what often holds us back . . .

5

• • •

Put Procrastination on Pause

I don't wait for moods. You accomplish nothing if you do that.
Your mind must know it has got to get down to work.

—PEARL S. BUCK, author and Nobel Prize winner

"I can always go for a walk tomorrow."

"I'm pretty busy getting caught up; I'll make some sales calls next week."

"Today isn't a good time; I'll apologize to her tomorrow."

"It's only one donut and, after all, I'm starting my diet this weekend."

"I'll call later in the day, when I have more time."

Sound familiar?

Admit it: you procrastinate . . . and I procrastinate—we all do. But my experience has been that it rarely serves me.

The word procrastinate is formed from two Latin words—*pro*, meaning 'forward', and *crastinus*, meaning 'belonging to tomorrow'. So, procrastination is the act of putting something into tomorrow and, of course, it suggests that the something is *always* 'in tomorrow'—in other words, it never gets done.

We pay our taxes late and are penalized, even though last year we swore we wouldn't. We put off starting the diet because it's 'not a good time', or because everyone else ordered the cheesecake with fresh strawberries. We fuss with the minutiae of designing the meeting agenda, instead of returning the calls from customers, and then blame that same customer for shopping around for new quotes. Or we avoid being honest with the co-worker who interrupts our work to chat, because 'I don't want to hurt his feelings'.

We have a natural tendency to avoid the pain of hard work, to put it off, and to take the path of least resistance. This habit of procrastination can undermine all of our planning, team commitments, and good intentions.

And it is all in our head.

Just as you made up the idea that a task is important (of course the fourth email in capitals from your boss is pretty good evidence!), you can also make up the idea that it will take a lot of effort, or that maybe—if you avoid it—you won't have to do it. Essentially, procrastination is a story we tell ourselves to avoid perceived pain.

So the co-worker is oblivious to the irritation we feel when he comes by our desk to talk about last night's hockey game. We avoided the anticipated uncomfortable feeling that comes from sharing a little honesty, and now we get to relive the same interruption day after day.

Here's a mental re-frame for you: when you procrastinate, you are not actually idle. When you procrastinate you *are* doing something—it just happens to be the wrong thing. For example, when you slack off in the afternoon and spend an hour wading through unread emails even though that sales report (that you have yet to start) is due tomorrow, *you are still being active.* The path of least resistance won again.

It stands to reason that, if you are active when you procrastinate, the path to more success is to *simply redirect your activity to a better choice.*

When I return from a meeting, I am always tempted to try to hack away at the forty new emails that have come in since I left.

The reality is that most of these emails have little value—they're certainly not as important as my Day Plan.

Instead, I make a conscious decision to take only fifteen minutes to scan and respond to critical client emails, and then I turn my attention to working on the next Pebble from my Day Plan.[49]

It's simply about staying in motion with better choices.

Reducing the Big-P Temptation

Similarly, when I return to my hotel room after delivering a speech, I am usually spent. I've had a long day, given it my all on stage, spent time talking to dozens of people, and I just want to crash in front of the television and 'veg out'. But what if my plan was to get a workout at the gym? Even as I made that goal in the morning, I knew that the Big-P (procrastination) temptation would be there.

So instead, I trick my brain to choose the workout instead of TV. Before leaving my room, I lay out all my workout gear on the bed. That way, when I return to the room, I see my gear, remember my commitment, and head off to the gym. Remember, *I'm going to be active anyway*; I might as well be active on the right thing.

---

49. A great technique is to set an alarm for fifteen minutes. Many of the new phones have alarms built in, or see www.e.ggtimer.com

Procrastination is a habit, and the best antidote to habits that don't serve you well is to create better habits that do, to notice evidence that supports this change, and to then repeat the new habit.

Please don't read this as a lecture on positive thinking. As much as I am a fan of being an optimist and seeing the best in yourself, this is about *strategies*. Sometimes it takes more than a positive outlook to change a pattern we have had for years.

I'm going to suggest seven proven strategies that you can employ right now. I'm sure there are loads more, but these are the ones that I use, and I know that any one of them will turbocharge your activities by reducing the Big-P temptation.

As always, you need to commit to at least one of these for a minimum of thirty days, and notice any differences in your results. This isn't about *perfect*; it is about gradual improvement that gets you more of what you want.

- **Take responsibility for each delay.** When you catch yourself procrastinating, add up the time you have spent thinking about starting that Pebble or Boulder. Now ask yourself what one change in your thinking or actions would create better results. *Then take your own advice, and do it!*

  When I catch myself scanning my Day Plan and still not taking action, I recognize it for what it is—procrastination. My solution is to pick one quick win, do it, cross it off the list and then start another one. By staying in motion, from one success to another, my mood soon improves, as does my focus on completion.

- **Skip the perfection.** It doesn't have to be perfect (with exceptions, of course, for heart surgeons and airline pilots)—it just has to be good enough to get the work done and to satisfy those involved. When you catch yourself fussing over the exact timing on the agenda or margins on a report, remind yourself that you might be the only one who cares. Seeking perfection is just another form of procrastination, and when the meeting is over and the report is on the shelf, nobody cares.

- **Rewrite your negative beliefs.** When you find yourself slipping into old, negative self-talk, stop and restate what you are thinking as a positive affirmation of what you do well ("I *do* complete what I start," or "I enjoy working at my own pace, ahead of schedule."). Remember, a chorus of neurons are eavesdropping on your mental machinations, and being programmed. You are your biggest cheerleader, and sometimes even a cheerleader needs coaching.

- **Chunking.** Break down projects into manageable pieces that can be accomplished in short amounts of time. Even fifteen minutes is enough time to rough out a table of contents for your new report, book a meeting room, send a query note to a colleague, or review a proposal.

  I like to think in terms of moving Boulders ahead with small pushes done frequently, rather than waiting for the perfect time to do it all. Building your successes effectively rewrites your story, from someone who avoids hard work, to someone who gets things done.

- **Do the most difficult task first.** You know that procrastinating on important work has a nasty habit of coming back to bite you. Instead, highlight the most important tasks in your Day Plan, and start to work on them first thing in the morning. Plan to tackle the most difficult tasks in high-energy time zones and to leave the less-taxing work for low-energy zones.

- **Reward yourself.** Your brain learns best through experience, so give it good ones to record. Give yourself a reward for starting the project, and for every milestone you reach. It could be a favorite brew at the local café, sitting outside reading for a few minutes, or hanging out in the staff room. Yes, it's mental coercion, but it works.

- **Create an un-schedule.** Psychologist Neil Fiore suggests mapping out your week, showing all the commitments you have. What is left is your 'un-schedule', where you can schedule down time, reading time, research or writing time. The un-schedule will help you to be realistic and to prepare for the chunks of time where you need to be focused. It may be that you only have two or three time blocks available, so it's important to prepare to make the most of what time you have.

Now that we've looked at your productivity habits, you're ready to get unproductive!

6

• • •

Make Time for Me-Time

Each of us needs some time that is entirely our own . . .
Just make sure your time alone is not interrupted
by your To-Do list, or anyone else's.

—STEPHAN RECHTSCHAFFEN, author
and co-founder of the Omega Center

"If I get to pee twice, it's a good day."

That's how the division director of a national investment firm described her typical day. Scheduled and impromptu meetings, panicked consultants needing her attention, and calls from her own clients usually packed every available minute.

At the end of a crazy-busy day of returning phone calls, responding to emails, and putting out fires, I sometimes feel that I'm on a treadmill, with no end in sight. It's ironic. All our efforts to do things faster so we will have more time often leaves us feeling burnt out and time-poor. As comedian Lily Tomlin so brilliantly put it: "The problem with the rat race, is that even if you win, you are still a rat."

Stephan Rechtschaffen, co-founder of the pioneering self-development Omega Institute in Rhinebeck, New York, wrote eloquently about the need for us to resist becoming an ultra-efficient 'doing machine' in his book, *Timeshifting.* "The time management taught at business seminars is essentially designed to make you more materially productive," warned Rechtschaffen. "If God could take the seventh day off to rest, then a half-hour a day doesn't seem much to ask of ourselves."

Here is a quick exercise—read the following list, and put a checkmark beside the descriptions you might use sometimes to describe yourself at work:

- Other people's agendas are driving my day.

- My typical day is so chaotic and unpredictable that my plans quickly become meaningless.

- Interruptions run my life; I have a hard time finding five minutes for myself.

- I feel guilty if I'm not always busy.

- As soon as I finish one task or meeting, I always go straight into another.

- I feel like I am on a treadmill, and the days don't seem to change or improve.

- I find I am checking email on my BlackBerry at restaurants and at home, when I should be enjoying time off.

- I know I should be taking more time to think and plan, but I don't.

- I work through the weekend; it's the only time when I can finally get work done.

- I notice my attention span is getting shorter, and I'm having trouble focusing for more than a few minutes.

- The only quiet time I get is in the washroom.

As you added your check marks, did you feel the need for change growing? Constantly going faster, packing more into your day, and rushing from task to task is not a recipe for success.

Instead, I like to create what I call 'Me-Time' in my day. Me-Time is like a pit stop; it is your opportunity to slow down, take stock, recharge, and get focused for what lies ahead. You can use it to do nothing and relax, or to read a favorite blog. This is your time to use in a way that will make the next hour, and the one after that, more effective and more enjoyable.

Sometimes, I use this time simply to get reoriented to my Action Plan for the week and to check on my plan for the rest of the day. Or I can use it for brainstorming and getting creative about some new direction I want to take the company. But more often than not, I use it to do nothing but relax into a meditative state, and quiet my thoughts.

Here are some simple ideas for how you can build Me-Time into your week:

Schedule Regular Me-Time

Regardless of the focus, you will have more success if you *schedule* Me-Time, rather than leaving it to the whims of attitude or the mercy of others. I know scheduling time for yourself may sound somewhat regimented, but ask yourself how many times you *intended* to take a break in the day, but instead kept on working? In fact, a colleague once commented that most people are never late for a meeting with another person, but they will often skip a meeting with themselves. It's time to change that prioritization.

Maybe a little discipline is not such a bad thing once in a while.

Remember the financial planner who told me he didn't take appointments on Thursday afternoons? Rather than hoping some free time would appear, he actually blocked research time into his schedule. We should all do the same.

My technique is to schedule at least thirty minutes (one hour is better) of Me-Time every week in my Action Plan. When you do this, be specific about the goal you want to work on and set the time, just like a meeting you might book with a client. It can be in smaller chunks, but it should add up to at least thirty minutes.

Let others know that this is a meeting you are booked for, and do not let anyone override it.[50] By scheduling this time, you send an important message to your subconscious that you are important enough to have time just for you.

Book Yourself Out of the Office

To create Me-Time, I often cross the street to a café, order a tea, let my mind relax, and take my attention off unfinished work.

I don't take my cell phone—just my laptop.[51] The only commitment I make is that I will focus on just one Pebble that needs my attention, and that I will reach some kind of conclusion. For

---

50. One client of mine color-codes her Me-Time by using categories in Outlook Calendar. This way, her staff and colleagues know what is negotiable time, in case of emergencies.

51. One trick I have learned is to not go online. First, you can easily lose fifteen minutes fooling around with café passwords and WiFi connections, and second, going online invites the distractions of email and Internet. Resist the habit, avoid the distraction, and get something done you'll be proud of.

example, I might edit a chapter in this book, work on a new feature for my website, do some committee work, make notes on a draft proposal, or do a mind map for a new project.

I look forward to these little escapes; they make me feel more productive, even though I am only working on one thing. And I return to my office feeling refreshed and refocused.

Take a Me-Time Walk

As an avid runner, I know that physical activity of any kind stimulates centers in our brain that allow for creative thought and a more positive mood. A brisk walk of even fifteen minutes will increase your heart rate, release endorphins that reduce pain, and give you a feeling of well-being. Heading out for a quick four-block tour in the middle of the day can turn around your dull feeling of work pressure, and return you to the office feeling more positive and focused.

> *When you're on top of everything it's hard to get to the bottom of anything.*
> —LINDA STONE, who coined the phrase "continuous partial attention"

In his book, *Walking Your Blues Away: How to Heal the Mind and Create Emotional Well-Being*, Thom Hartman promotes the value of walking for changing the emotional energy around a problem and for finding new solutions. He recommends that you choose one topic or challenge, and stay focused on it throughout your walk. When you find yourself drifting off topic, remind yourself to refocus on that one topic.

As you walk, notice how your issue begins to morph and change. It could be a subtle change in feeling or a new solution could begin to bubble to the surface. Toward the end of your walk, anchor your new feeling or solution by recording the new direction or action you are going to take.

I was doing this one day as I ruminated about a staffing issue.

I had just received notice that my main employee was going on maternity leave—permanently. She was the glue that held together hundreds of details, and her departure would be a huge loss.

The usual remedies started to come up: replace her, look at temp services, etc. As I walked, I allowed these knee-jerk solutions to quiet, and I chose instead to just be with the question: "What do I really want?" It was freeing to not jump into solution-creating mode. I started to notice the walk more, taking in the fresh air, enjoying the physical movement, and feeling my feet as they carried me into a nearby park.

> *If you're not getting better, you're getting worse.*
> —PAT RILEY, philosopher and NBA coach

After about ten minutes, the thought of replacing her began taking a back seat to envisioning my ideal day—what I really wanted. I started to picture simpler surroundings at work, with less paper and fewer filing cabinets, and fewer wires and boxes humming away doing who-knows-what. It was freeing!

By the time I returned to my office, I was convinced that the solution was not about replacing my employee; it was about becoming free of the complexity of my current office set-up. Within a few days and with her help, we had crafted a plan to move the company to a one-person office. We also drafted a new work plan for the operation of the company, and began actively outsourcing as much work as possible.

I'm convinced that none of these solutions would have come to me if I had stayed in my office making lists. I needed to break free from my usual patterns of problem-solving and to ask a different set of questions.

It only took ten minutes of walking to get the process started, but it opened a new world for my company. Two weeks later, virtually all the unnecessary furniture, phones, fax machine, and computers were either sold or given to charity. I also hauled more than twelve huge bags of old files, records, reports, and paper out of the office to be recycled. It was like a metaphor for mental clarity: the more paper that was removed, the freer my thinking became.

The moral of the story is: When in doubt, take a hike.

By the way, walking is also a wonderful alternative to a traditional sitting meeting. I have found that there can be less tension, more positive energy, and even more honesty in a walking meeting.

Bust out of Busy-ness

If you've ever watched someone arrive at a café, order their food and drink, get to a table, open their laptop and get out their phone, hook up to the WiFi, start checking their email, all while eating their food, you know what busy-ness looks like. Busy-ness is a disease of our always-on culture—that keeps us away from simply being present. It's most evident in places like airport lounges, hotel lobbies, office elevators, bus stops, and other public places. But it also happens while people are driving their car, on the phone, or at home with their partner or family.

Here's an exercise that you might find both challenging and quite revealing: do nothing. Go to a bookstore, café, or any public space, and simply sit quietly and just be there. Avoid the temptation to check email, make a call, or read the paper; just be present, and take in what is going on all around you and inside you.

I know, if my mind is full of thoughts from the day at work, it can be a challenge to slow down and just be present. The temptation is to click, type, read, list, or do anything to keep busy and feed my anxious, distracted mind. In fact, in that moment doing nothing more than breathing and observing may be the most productive activity I can choose.

Create mini Me-Time Breaks

We often treat our days as a series of highlights—
the big meeting, a good meal, an outing with the kids—
while ignoring the time in between. But the
in-between moments are the bulk of our lives.

–THICH NHAT HANH, author and peace activist

When the workload is up and your Day Plan is bulging with demands on your time, you can use these simple techniques to create mini Me-Time breaks throughout the day:

- When the phone rings, use that as a cue to relax. Take a deep breath, center your focus on only that moment, release any anxiety or worries, and allow your thoughts to quiet. It only takes a moment, but it can make a world of difference—to you, and to how you sound on the call.

- Instead of rushing to arrive on time to meetings or appointments, plan to arrive five minutes early. Use this free time to compose your thoughts, update your Day Plan, or review the meeting agenda. Do this and you may notice that, for the first ten minutes, you are one of the few people who is grounded and thinking clearly.

- After you finish one task, pause for a moment before beginning another. One habit I have picked up this year is to enjoy a mini-celebration after a particularly difficult task has been accomplished. I just take a moment to stand and stretch, to reflect on what was accomplished, and to feel pride for overcoming my procrastination habit and getting it done. It doesn't have to be a big deal, but allow your conscious mind a moment to register and connect good feelings with your extra effort.

- Stay focused on the present. While waiting for a website to load up, your computer to reboot, an elevator to arrive, or a light to turn green, simply notice what is going on around you and inside you.

  Are you tense? How is your breathing? What are your thoughts? The act of focusing will bring you to a new level of awareness. You will find you are less scattered in your thinking and more attuned to the task at hand, or to the person you are with.

You are the author of your day—if you choose to be. Or as mega-author, Wayne Dyer puts it, "Our lives are the sum total of the choices we make." The trick, it seems, is to make more conscious choices that are designed to create more success for us and others, rather than unconscious choices based on habit, fear, or resistance.

And now that you are pumped to make more conscious choices, how about choosing to get some things off your list?

7

●　●　●

Start a Stop-Doing List

Civilization had too many rules for me,
so I did my best to rewrite them.

–BILL COSBY, comedian

For at least twenty years, I have been signing checks. In every business I have started or managed, it was just one of those responsibilities that went with the territory, or so I thought. After all, shouldn't the boss have ultimate responsibility for how the income was being spent?

About three years ago, on my return from a speaking tour, I took note of the stack of mail and invoices on my desk. It was substantial. Even though our regular bills (telephone, utilities, etc.) were paid automatically, there was still a small pile of envelopes on my desk every day awaiting my attention. Contractors needed to be paid, bills approved, staff paid, and so on. It would take me at least twenty to thirty minutes just to go through all the bills, write the checks, and then a few more minutes to file everything.

It was a distraction I didn't need and took time away from more client-focused tasks.

I decided to fight my habit and, for the first time, give my manager signing rights to our account. My plan was to create a prudent compromise: she would deal with items under $500, and I would sign off on larger items.

As we walked to the bank to sign the necessary signature cards, it dawned on me that setting such a low signing limit would still keep me busy, and didn't really demonstrate my trust in her. After all, if I trusted her to sign every small item, I should trust her to sign all of the checks.

So I decided to increase the limit to $1,500. Again, it was a compromise that still tied me to the process.

Finally, as we reached the doors of the bank, it dawned on me how dumb this was. Here I was, trying to get rid of responsibility, but still hanging on to it. It was time to not only delegate the task, but to give complete autonomy along with it.

So I removed the signing limit completely.

Now, with full authority to deal with any payment (on paper and online) delegated to my manager, I have a real solution. Not only have I reclaimed the time, this is one less task on my list and one less pile on my desk.[52] I should have done it ten years ago.

So far, we have covered a lot of material about what you can do to make time work for you. But what about what we don't need to do? Author Jim Collins once shared how to put a stop to work and responsibilities that you are not passionate about, are not genetically

---

52. I recognize that paying bills is one of the 'mundane tasks' I talked about previously. In this case, there was the added incentive to delegate some responsibility.

encoded for, or that don't make economic sense (or what I like to refer to as "Just-Plain-Dumb").[53]

Just-Plain-Dumb

Earnestness is stupidity sent to college.

-P. J. O'ROURKE, journalist and author

If you are ever going to truly increase your success, you need to first increase your capacity. Like trying to cram more clothes into an already full suitcase, there are always some non-negotiable limits on life. And those limits won't increase until you either buy a new suitcase (expensive) or reduce your pile of clothes (not always easy). Think of it this way: when you empty your 'must-do' vessel of real, assumed, or Just-Plain-Dumb obligations and duties, you naturally allow new and better opportunities to flow your way.

The 'must-do' disease plagued me for years, and I was continually filling my bucket of responsibilities faster than I could empty them. This never-ending cycle of complete-one, add-two-more tasks, often led to chaos, poor decisions, stress, and missed opportunities. When I was in survival mode all the time, I couldn't see, much less entertain, different, more selective, or strategic approaches.

But just like the feeling I get when I donate to charity clothes I haven't worn in years; when I purge unnecessary, or unwanted tasks, it is like a weight has been lifted off my shoulders. My thinking is less encumbered and set free to contemplate new and better directions.

Now consider your habits: are you a 'doer', grinding away without reprieve at a self-created mountain of work and responsibilities? Or are you growing your capacity by doing less to get more?

---

53. http://www.jimcollins.com/article_topics/articles/best-new-years.html

Doing Less to Get More

Here is my current Stop-Doing list. Take what you want from it, and then create your own. Have fun with this. Look for repetitive tasks that either: someone else can do, doesn't need to be done, or you simply don't want ever see again. And then find a new solution for getting them off your list, permanently.

1) **Working through breaks.** It's a mind trick: you think that, if you work continuously, you get more done. Watch NBA or NHL players—how long could they perform at their best if they weren't taking breaks? Learn from the pros and use breaks to maximize your results.

2) **Being anchored to email.** Don't fill gaps in your day by checking your Inbox. No one is impressed, and you are just keeping yourself busy instead of productive. Remember, "Those who don't have goals are ruled by those who do." If email is your vice, you have given your power over to the sender (re-read the chapter "Exorcise Your Email").

3) **Worrying.** Don't get me wrong—I pay attention to what's important, and at times I become concerned about what needs to be changed, but I avoid worry. Repeatedly worrying about what might or might not happen is a wasted investment. If I screwed up, I'll deal with it. In the meantime, I choose to live more in the present. We always have a choice; I choose to not worry.

4) **Seeking perfection.** The first iPod was far from perfect, yet Apple now owns more than 70% of the world portable music market share. It's the same for any success story. Perfection is a luxury that should be pursued by musicians, rocket scientists, and surgeons; all the rest of us should be interested in client satisfaction, profit, growth, and (we hope) personal fulfillment and reward.

5) **Faking delegation.** It's counter-intuitive, but people want more responsibility and autonomy; they just don't always show it. Get out of your own way and pass the ropes over to the person who should be doing the work. You will be free to work on more important things and they will be happier campers.[54]

6) **Needing to finish books and magazines.** There are over 23,000 new books published every month in the US alone—does it really matter that you didn't finish one of them? Here's my rule of thumb: if it's taking me longer than a week to finish the book, it's either not good enough, not interesting enough, or I don't need it enough.

7) **Procrastinating about health.** It's no wonder that one out of four men, and one out of three women, who survive a heart attack will die within the following year, most often of cardiac arrest or another heart attack—they are still procrastinating about their health. Staying healthy takes less effort and time than you think. Make it easy, convenient, and fun, and make it a habit as soon as possible.

8) **Bringing work home.** Set aside days of the week that are *No Guilt Days*. No work comes home, and you enjoy total family time and down-time. You will be more refreshed and ready for the next day, and have less guilt (most nights you don't do all that you planned anyway).

9) **Staying busy.** It's hard to be strategic if you're crazy-busy all the time. I choose to enjoy breaks during the day, to have my evenings for myself and my family, and to not always take on more projects.

---

54. Daniel Pink's new best-seller, *Drive: The Surprising Truth About What Motivates Us,* reveals some surprising reasons why some people perform, and many others never do.

10) **Reading the news.** In a ten-day study, researchers recorded both negative and positive statements used in the evening news. Not surprisingly, they found there were more negative statements than positive ones in every broadcast; in fact, ten times more. So why—as you start your day or as you are winding down in the evening—would you want to hear what's going wrong in the world? Instead, I have a solution: if you want to know what is going on in the world, guess—you're probably right.

It's amazing that the amount of news that happens
in the world every day always just exactly fits the newspaper.
–JERRY SEINFELD, comedian

Some other things to commit to Stop-Doing are:

- Watching excessive TV

- Spending every evening at home on the computer

- Chairing meetings that someone else could chair

- Attending meetings you don't really need to be at

- Over-eating, or eating food that you know doesn't serve you

- Constantly checking, emailing, and surfing on your phone

- Playing safe when sharing your opinions

- Working through breaks and skipping opportunities for Me-Time

- Saying 'Yes' before considering the impact on you and your family

- Getting stuck thinking you are right

8

• • •

Celebrate Successes

Celebrate good times, come on!

—KOOL & THE GANG, "Celebration"

Years ago, I created a little habit to celebrate exercising, and I continue it to this day (despite how strange it may sometimes look). After a run or a workout, as I am heading to the shower, I always reach across my left shoulder and give myself a little pat on the back. It is my way of saying, "You did it! You got your butt out the door and did what you said you would do."

Sometimes it feels a little strange to be executing my self-congratulatory ceremony as I walk through a public gym, but it's important to me. I want to reinforce my belief that I am a promise-keeper and that I make my health a priority. And the next time I am convincing myself to get ready for the workout, it will be just a little easier, because I know there is a small reward waiting for me.

Why is it that we don't celebrate more often?

We work hard, take risks, achieve success, and then quickly

move on to the next task. It seems that guilt plays a role in our dedication to staying busy and in our habit of reward avoidance. At some time in our life, we must have learnt that celebrating was either self-serving or unnecessary.

Well, that is exactly why we *should do it*—because it is self serving and unnecessary!

Once we finish the task or project, or overcome our resistance and accomplish what we set out to do, it is no longer about 'necessary'—it should be about relief, rejoicing, and restoring our faith in hard work and perseverance.

Imagine if a football team skipped the 'high fives' and bum slaps after a touchdown. Or how about a tennis player landing that perfect, out-of-reach corner shot, and not taking a moment to raise her fist in celebration?

It's important to remind ourselves that we are successful and that our hard work is paying off. Like a video camera that is always on, our brain constantly records and processes our experiences, and creates new synapse connections that record our version of what happened. Every experience either reinforces an existing connection (think of a well-established river stream where water naturally wants to flow) or creates a new one.

When you put in extra effort, but there is little reward, you reinforce the brain's 'story' that says work is unrewarding. This unconscious action-reaction response influences future decisions. Work? Ugh—there's no reward in hard work!

On the other hand, when you take a moment to savor the feeling of success after working hard, you program your brain to make a connection between working hard and feeling good. It's basic Skinner Stimulus-Response theory at work (without the rats in a maze).

However you choose to celebrate, be spontaneous, make it fun, and make it happen on a regular basis. Here are some ideas for how you can celebrate your own successes:

- Stop in the middle of the day, notice some specific accomplishments you have made (however minor in the big picture), and congratulate yourself.

- Cross each task off your list with a thick felt pen and enjoy seeing your Day-Timer fill up with signs of accomplishment.

- Go for a quick walk outside. Allow yourself to completely take your mind off work, focus on the experience of the walk, and simply enjoy the break.

- Indulge yourself with a favorite treat at a local café. But don't spend the time checking your emails—just enjoy the celebration.

- Reward yourself with a stretch. Remind yourself that this stretch represents your celebration and that you are enjoying the feeling of completing a task.

- Take ten minutes to read an article that you've been wanting to read, but haven't gotten around to. Stay focused, and enjoy single-tasking.

- Post the name of the Pebble with a red felt pen line through it on a sticky note and keep this visible for the day as a reminder of your progress.

- Take a few minutes and intentionally remove all the papers, files, and reminders of the task from sight. This is visual confirmation that you are moving on.

- Do nothing. A favorite 'celebration' for me is to move to my office couch, sit quietly, breath, and let my mind relax. As I release my thoughts from To-Do's I bring my attention to a peaceful, relaxing scene. Five minutes of quiet meditation relieves me of stress and worry and recharges me.

Habits Worksheet

New habits that stick include a commitment to practice them for at least thirty days. This means thinking about the new habit every day, consciously practicing it, and doing your best to stick with it.

I am committing to the following habit:

....

....

I am committing to the following habit:

....

....

I am committing to the following habit:

....

....

Here is how I am going to support myself in keeping this new habit: (e.g. I will put a note in my Day-Timer or on my home page, I will review my progress every afternoon as I plan the next day, I will reward myself by . . .)

....

....

....

....

Recommendations: Post copies of this page in your day planner, on your bathroom mirror, your car dashboard, or your refrigerator—any place where you will see it frequently and be reminded of your commitments. You can download copies of all the chapter worksheets at www.hugh culver.com/breakbook

Part IV

• • •

THIS IS THE TIME

Committing to your success

Here you leave today and enter the world of yesterday, tomorrow, and fantasy.

–Message greeting visitors to Disneyland

It Doesn't Stop Here

In a quarterly retreat I was leading with a group of high-achieving managers, I asked for a show of hands: "How many of you have more distractions from interruptions, crises, emails, staff, conflicting time demands, and meetings than you had one year ago?"

With a collective groan, all thirty-three hands went up.

Next, I asked who had adopted a specific new strategy this year to reduce these distractions. Only four hands went up. Not taking time to improve when the problem is obvious and growing is like frantically trying to bail out a leaking boat with a tea cup. Your efforts, while impressive, are barely keeping up with the leak, and you still haven't fixed the problem.

I've designed this book to provide tools that I know will work for you, so you can create more success with your time. But (sorry) it doesn't stop there. To gain the maximum benefit from this knowledge, you also have to commit to an *attitude of continuous improvement.* The

Beliefs
Habits
Continuous Improvement
Goals
Systems

ongoing process of awareness, reflection, change, and commitment is the source of all real improvement.

Imagine being part of a business that never changed or improved. Feedback from clients was ignored, errors were often repeated, and inefficiencies were overlooked. Of course it's a disastrous strategy!

We need to continually learn and discover new ways to do this thing called 'work'. I want this book to challenge you to find efficiencies you didn't enjoy before and to rethink old assumptions.

> *If your actions inspire others to dream more, learn more, do more and become more, you are a leader.*
>
> –JOHN QUINCY ADAMS, sixth president of the United States

Every week, when you are creating your new Action Plan, take a few minutes for your own weekly review. This doesn't have to be a complete analysis; just look for what worked (how can I repeat this?) and what didn't work (how can I avoid that the next time?).

Here are three powerful questions to ask yourself every week:

1) Where have I succeeded this week, and what can I do to repeat that success? (Think about a system opportunity.)

2) Where have I missed the mark this week? This could include being unprepared or late to a meeting, or missing a deadline. (Think about a new habit opportunity.)

3) Where do I need to improve? This could include being more disciplined about sticking to your Day Plan in the morning, or blocking more time to work on your Boulders. (Think about a new learning opportunity.)

That Feeling of Déjà Vu

It is a miracle that curiosity survives formal education.

—CHET ATKINS, country recording artist

Do you ever have a stressful week, and then recognize that this week is probably no different from the previous week? Your feeling of déjà vu is a clue worth paying attention to. A pattern of frustration, stress, or just plain fatigue means that there is an opportunity and a need to create a better approach.

Scott is a successful mortgage broker with a growing business. He makes his money by attracting individual home buyers and closing their mortgage deals. And in his business, it's all about numbers. The more Scott can apply his time to finding new clients and processing mortgage applications, the more success he enjoys.

But Scott was constantly frustrated by the tedious, detailed, and time-consuming application forms. Week after week, Scott's sales success was being stymied by the administration of the applications. Working harder wasn't working! The solution seemed to be about doing less of the wrong work and more of what Scott was best suited for—attracting new business.

First, he made a list, detailing all the steps required to process a mortgage application, either manually or online. Next, he placed a help-wanted ad for assistance three days a week from 9:30 am to 2:30 pm (a perfect time for stay-at-home mothers with school-age children). Despite offering a relatively low wage, he was flooded with enquiries from young mothers who wanted to earn some extra income, but on their schedule. A part-time staff person was hired and trained, and Scott has never looked back.

Your time-success (happiness, prosperity, family-time, and personal fulfillment) is simply a reflection of the decisions you make every day. Noticing opportunities and then making those improvements, however minor at the time, can lead to surprising rewards and sooner than you might think. Like getting into a habit of de-cluttering your workspace, updating your Day Plan, and celebrating your successes can lead to huge rewards with little extra effort.

Which one of these areas will you focus on?

- **How you organize meetings** – Is there wasted, unproductive time that frustrates you? Are you getting the results you want? If they were invited to openly share feedback, what would your team members say?

- **How you learn** – Do the latest self-help or business books litter your bedroom, but rarely seem to result in meaningful change? Are you spending endless hours reading blogs, articles, and e-zines without seeing any measurable benefit? Maybe you need to cancel some subscriptions, practice speed reading, experiment with podcasts or audio books, and commit to making at least one change from every book you invest in.

- **How you manage your energy** – Have you made any improvements recently to better manage your energy in the day? Have you looked at replacing some high-sugar snacks with healthier options? Try this simple daily commitment for one month: drink more water—starting with first thing in the morning, take two walking breaks, and intentionally stand and move between tasks. As high performance expert, Dr. Jim Loehr instructs: "You can only expend as much energy as you create."

- **How you manage interruptions** – Are you honest with people when you really don't have time? Do you return to your Action Plan after interruptions, or are you 'pinballing' to other tasks that grab your attention? You might need to practice blocking time, saying 'No', and closing the real or proverbial door to your work space more often.

Continuous improvement can be as simple as learning a shortcut key in M/S Outlook, or more complex, like delegating entire tasks to someone else. It's all about sanity; trying new solutions until you get more of what you are looking for.

And it all starts by asking the questions: "What is not working?" and "What will I improve this week?"

It is Time

An ounce of performance is worth pounds of promises.

—MAE WEST, comedian, actress, and writer

How did you approach this book? Did you work your way through the chapter exercises, or breeze by those pages and rush off to the next chapter? Maybe you experimented with making some changes as you were reading the chapters. Or maybe you wanted to get all the information and *then* decide on your plan (notice that I'm not giving you the 'Do Nothing' option?).

My guess is that, in over 50,000 words, there had to be something that got your attention, has value, and could be put into action.

Here's the bottom line: reading and doing nothing is no better than not reading the book at all.

If, on the other hand, you make one change now that saves you some twenty minutes a day, and stick with it, that's the equivalent of two full weeks of recovered time.

That's fantastic! That new-found time is yours to use for health, reading, cleaning up clutter, or whatever. And, best of all, it is time that you created—you tackled the systems, changed the habits, and made the change.

Still not committed? Here is a quick review, to refresh your memory, and to get you thinking about the value you will take from this book.

Beliefs – Believe that you are the master of your time, and not the victim of other people's agendas. When you find yourself procrastinating, or running frantically from meeting to email to meeting again, notice the recurring thoughts that percolate up. Remind yourself of what you do well, and ask yourself, "What is one change I can make immediately that will move me closer to where I want to be with my time?" Focus on that new answer and let the nagging doubts dissolve in the more powerful belief.

> *Only dead fish go with the current all the time.*
> —LINDA ELLERBEE, journalist

Goals – Goals are where it all begins; your determination, direction, and destiny all start with your goals. Have career and life goals that excite you, and that get you out of bed in the morning. Don't hold back—if you aren't stretched by your goals, there's no motivation to reach them. *Remember: Those who don't have goals are ruled by those who do.*

Systems – Improve your systems, and reap the benefits every day and every year. Maybe your meetings are dysfunctional or your paperwork has a life of its own. Think about these changes as investments in your health. One small improvement now to your meetings, your paper management, or your email, will reward you long-term with better work-health. You can get more work done with less effort and less stress. That's healthy.

Habits – You are a creature of habit. This can either work for you or against you. The trick is to be aware of your habits and to be selective about which ones you keep. It's actually a fun exercise to just notice habits for one week. Keep a journal and note all the habits that pop up as you go through your day. Then make a choice to change the ones that don't serve you.

Continuous Improvement – Here are two great questions to ask yourself every day: "Am I living up to my potential?" and "What one change do I need to make to create more value right now?" Continuous improvement is all about awareness, asking good questions, and making small changes in the right direction—even if that change is just in the way you think.

How you experience your day and work is always up to you. It may seem as though the events going on around you—including other people and their crises—have the upper hand. But in fact, through your beliefs, goals, systems, and habits, you always hold the trump card—the question is whether you will choose to play it.

You are the author of your day. Now it's up to you to write your story the way you want.

Recommended Reading

These are books that I trust and have learned from; any one of them is an asset. You can use this list to find the ones best suited to help you learn more about the art of making time work for you.

Allen, David. (2009). *Making It All Work: Winning at the Game of Work and the Business of Life.* New York: Penguin Books.

Autry, James A. (1996). *Confessions of an Accidental Businessman: It Takes a Lifetime to Find Wisdom.* New York: Random House.

Covey, Stephen, with A. Roger and Rebecca R. Merrill. (1994). *First Things First: To Live, to Love, to Learn, to Leave a Legacy.* New York: Simon and Schuster.

Dyer, Dr. Wayne W. (2010). *The Shift: Taking Your Life from Ambition to Meaning.* Hay House.

Emmerich, Roxanne. (2009). *Thank God It's Monday!: How to Create a Workplace You and Your Customers Love.* FT Press.

Ferriss, Timothy. (2007). *The 4-Hour Workweek: Escape 9–5, Live Anywhere, and Join the New Rich.* New York: Crown Publishing.

Frankl, Viktor E. (1962). *Man's Search for Meaning: An Introduction to Logotherapy.* Boston: Beacon Press.

Fried, Jason and David Heinemeier Hansson. (2010). *Rework.* Crown Business.

Fritz, Robert. (1989). *Path of Least Resistance: Learning to Become the Creative Force in Your Own Life.* New York: Ballantine Books.

Hallowell, Edward. M. (2006). *CrazyBusy: Overstretched, Over-booked, and About to Snap!* New York: Ballantine Books.

Hartman, Thom. (2006). *Walking Your Blues Away: How to Heal the Mind and Create Emotional Well-Being.* Park Street Press.

Loehr, Jim and Tony Schwartz. (2004). *The Power of Full Engagement: Managing Energy, Not Time, Is the Key to High Performance and Personal Renewal.* Free Press.

Merrill, Douglas and James A. Martin. (2010). *Getting Organized in the Google Era: How to Get Stuff out of Your Head, Find It When You Need It, and Get It Done Right.* Crown Business.

Morgenstern, Julie. (2004). *Time Management from the Inside Out, Second Edition: The Foolproof System for Taking Control of Your Schedule—and Your Life.* Holt Paperbacks.

Pink, Daniel H. (2009). *Drive: The Surprising Truth About What Motivates Us.* Riverhead Hardcover.

Pressfield, Steven. (2003). *The War of Art: Break Through the Blocks and Win Your Inner Creative Battles.* Grand Central Publishing.

Rechtschaffen, Stephan. (1997). *Timeshifting: Creating More Time to Enjoy Your Life.* Main Street Books.

Restak, Richard. (2002). *Mozart's Brain and the Fighter Pilot: Unleashing Your Brain's Potential.* Three Rivers Press.

Rock, David. (2009). *Your Brain at Work: Strategies for Overcoming Distraction, Regaining Focus, and Working Smarter All Day Long.* New York: Harper Business.

Snead, G. Lynne and Joyce Wycoff. (1997). *To Do Doing Done: A Creative Approach to Managing Projects & Effectively Finishing What Matters Most.* Fireside.

Stack, Laura. (2010). *SuperCompetent: The Six Keys to Perform at Your Productive Best.* Wiley.

Stanley, Thomas J. and William D. Danko. (1996). *The Millionaire Next Door: The Surprising Secrets of America's Wealthy.* Pocket Books.

About the Author

Hugh D. Culver, MBA, CSP

H ugh has been presenting his special blend of street smarts, humor, and passion since 1991 to more than 450 business organizations, and to universities and colleges. The owner of Marathon Communications, a corporate training company, he has an MBA degree, is a Certified Speaking Professional and Certified Facilitation Professional.

Hugh spent fifteen years as a professional whitewater guide and manager of the largest adventure travel company in Western Canada. With his brother Dan, he pioneered whitewater rafting adventures in British Columbia and eco-sailing tours of the Queen Charlotte Islands. Hugh also co-founded Adventure Network International, the world's only tourism company operating on the Antarctic continent.

In addition to his training work, Hugh launched the largest *Spirit in the Workplace* conference in Canada for business leaders, as well as the *Dare2Dream* youth leadership sea kayaking program on the west coast of British Columbia.

Hugh also likes to create big wins in his personal life. He is a four-time Ironman competitor, ten-time marathoner, past demonstration skier, and nationally ranked whitewater kayaking competitor. He has climbed the highest peaks in Canada and the United States, held the running record for the Chilkoot Pass Trail in the Yukon, and golfed at the North Pole.

Hugh lives in Kelowna, British Columbia, Canada with his wife, Kirsten, and their two daughters.

To inquire about having Hugh speak at your event or to order copies of this book, please contact our office at 1.800.313.0799 or info@hughculver.com.